THE SEDUCTION OF OUR CHILDREN

Neil T. Anderson & Steve Russo

HARVEST HOUSE PUBLISHERS
Eugene, Oregon 97402

Except where otherwise indicated, all Scripture quotations in this book are taken from the New American Standard Bible, © 1960, 1962, 1963, 1968, 1971, 1972, 1973, 1975, 1977 by The Lockman Foundation. Used by permission.

Verses marked NIV are taken from the Holy Bible, New International Version, Copyright © 1973, 1978, 1984 by the International Bible Society. Used by permission of Zondervan Bible Publishers.

Verses marked TLB are taken from The Living Bible © 1971 owned by assignment by Illinois Regional Bank N.A. (as trustee). Used by permission of Tyndale House Publishers, Inc., Wheaton, IL 60189. All rights reserved.

> The names of certain persons mentioned in this book have been changed in order to protect the privacy of the individuals involved.

THE SEDUCTION OF OUR CHILDREN

Copyright © 1991 by Harvest House Publishers
Eugene, Oregon 97402

Library of Congress Cataloging-in-Publication Data

Anderson, Neil T., 1942-
    Seduction of our children / Neil Anderson, Steve Russo.
    ISBN 0-89081-888-6
    1. Demonology.   2. Satanism.   3. Children—United
States—Religious life.   4. Parenting—Religious aspects—Christianity.   I. Russo, Steve, 1953-   II. Title.
BT981.A534   1991   91-3100
235.'4—dc20   CIP

All rights reserved. No portion of this book may be reproduced in any form without the written permission of the Publisher.

Printed in the United States of America.

We dedicate this book to our children:
Heidi and Karl Anderson
and
Tony and Kati Russo.

CONTENTS

XXXXXXXXXXXXXXXXXXXXXXXXXXXXXXXXXXXXXXXXXXXXXXXXXXXXXXXXXXXXXXXXXXXXXXXXXXXXX

Someone Is After Your Child

SOMEONE IS AFTER YOUR CHILD

Late one Saturday evening a pastor friend called me in desperation over his 14-year-old daughter. "Neil, Kelly has run away again." This pastor and his wife were godly parents. They had other children who were exemplary Christians. As I drove to their home that night I wondered why Kelly lived in such rebellion. I asked God to give me insight for helping this hurting couple and their troubled daughter.

When I arrived we shed a few tears, talked, and prayed together. Then I asked to see Kelly's room. I expected to see the dark posters and chaos that so often typify rebellious teenagers. But her parents wouldn't let Kelly keep her room that way. They had set limits to her personal expressions, which only seemed to upset her more. Kelly's room was like her life—on the edge. It barely met the minimum standards imposed by her parents. Kelly had also been testing the limits of her parents' discipline in her behavior and occasionally stepping over the line. This was one of those times.

I said, "I would like to talk to Kelly when she gets home. I sense that there is something spiritually wrong."

The father answered, "I would love for you to see Kelly. But if there is a demonic problem, wouldn't we be able to sense it?"

"Maybe not," I responded. "You're too emotionally involved as her parents. Besides, you're dealing with major deception from the enemy."

Within a couple of days Kelly came back home, and her father brought her to my office.

"I know these last few years have been difficult for you," I expressed to Kelly. "Can you share with me what's going on inside?"

"It's like I have a subconscious self talking to me," Kelly answered.

"One?" I asked.

"No, maybe two," she said.

I asked her if she would be willing to read through a prayer for spiritual freedom. She wasn't excited about it, but she said she would do it. She started to read the prayer, then stopped abruptly. Startled, she said, "I can't say this prayer!"

"Why not?" I asked.

"Because they're angry. They don't want me to read it."

"Who do you think they are?"

"I don't know," she responded. She really didn't know, so she had assumed for years that the thoughts plaguing her were her own. Whenever they told her to run away, she obeyed. Then in a few days she would come to her senses and return home. There seemed to be no escape from the voices that prompted her rebellious lifestyle.

I explained to Kelly that the inner voices were Satan's attempt to seduce her away from obedience to God and to her parents. I told her that she didn't have to listen to the voices anymore. She could be free. Within a week she changed schools and friends, and the following summer she went on a short-term missions trip. She was finally free.

You may be surprised to learn that there are many Christian children and teenagers like Kelly populating our schools, attending our churches, and living in our homes. They hear inner "voices" telling them that nobody loves them, urging them to disobey their parents, and disrupting their attempts at Bible reading and prayer.

They are the targets of Satan's strategy. He seeks to destroy our families and churches by seducing our children away from their parents and from God.

Are we saying that every evil thought in our mind is the "voice" of Satan or a demon? No, the flesh—that part of our brain that urges us to operate independent of God and to center our interests on ourselves—also introduces sinful thoughts and suggests evil deeds. Furthermore, input from worldly movies, music, books, TV, etc. also introduces evil ideas into our minds. As we grow in Christ we learn to say no to the deeds of the flesh and to walk in the Spirit.

But the world and the flesh are not the only culprits, even though we tend to place most of the blame on them. The devil and "spiritual forces of wickedness" (Ephesians 6:12) are shrewdly at work introducing evil suggestions as thoughts or inner voices. Just as we learn to deal with worldly and fleshly influences, so we must learn to distinguish Satan's subtle, personal influence and resist him, and we must teach our children to do the same. Whether your child's evil thoughts are coming from the world, the flesh, or the devil, this book will help you help him bring "every thought captive to the obedience of Christ" (2 Corinthians 10:5).

One of my seminary students was the father of three children. His middle son, normally the most pious of the three, developed a problem with lying and stealing items from the home. Dad and Mom disciplined him for his actions, but the more they disciplined him the more he stole and lied.

During one discipline session the little boy finally blurted out, "Daddy, I had to do those things. If I didn't, the devil said he would kill you!"

His father later told me, "If I hadn't heard your teaching about the battle for the mind, I would have doubled my son's discipline for blaming the devil for his behavior. Instead I explained to him that Satan was telling him lies in order to control his life and destroy our family. After we took a stand against the enemy, our son had one minor repeat a week later, then never again."

Our kids aren't saying much about Satan's seduction in their lives because most of them don't know that he's at the heart of it. Satan is the great deceiver. He doesn't march into their lives accompanied by a brass band. He slyly worms his way in through the opportunities they and we give him. And since kids haven't been taught what the Bible says about Satan's strategies, they blame themselves, and their sense of guilt and fear of punishment further contributes to their silence.

What are parents, Sunday school teachers, youth workers, and pastors to do in the face of this assault? Let's begin by stating what we can't do.

First, we can't bury our heads in the sand. This is not the time to respond in denial or claim that our Christian kids are immune to this kind of a problem. Satan's seductive activities are aimed at destroying the church at its point of greatest vulnerability: the family. The enemy is after Christian families in general and the families of Christian leaders in particular. Half of all my counseling regarding demonic influence is with Christian leaders and their families.

Second, we can't run in fear. Remember: Thanks to the death and resurrection of Jesus Christ, Satan is a defeated foe. The war against the seduction of our children is a winnable war. If we retreat instead of advance, we forfeit ground to the enemy that doesn't belong to him. We must exert our authority in Jesus Christ and claim His victory in the lives of our children.

How can we do that? Steve Russo and I have discussed

this question at length from the perspective of our different ministries. The Steve Russo Evangelistic Team is an international ministry to youth and their families. Steve travels the U.S. and the world reaching families for Christ through kids. He deals with thousands of kids each year who are influenced by New Age, Satanism, and the occult. And in my counseling, writing, and speaking over the last 17 years, I have ministered to thousands of parents and young people who were in bondage to demonic influence until they found their freedom in Christ. Steve and I have come up with three ways to defuse Satan's weapons of seduction aimed at our kids.

First, we must become aware of the spiritual nature of the world we live in. Our children are growing up in a seductive world. Many of the things that surround them are subtly influenced by the New Age movement, the occult, or Satanism. In Part One of this book we will analyze how Satan's influence in the world is behind many of the spiritual conflicts our children face.

Second, we need to understand how parents and parenting styles can either assist or block the resolution of a child's spiritual conflicts. If a child comes from a dysfunctional home, it's rather pointless to deal with his problem only to send him back into the home that caused his problem in the first place. In Part Two we will address the topic of parental identity and self-worth, styles of parenting, and the parenting skills of communication and discipline.

Third, we need definite strategies for protecting our children from spiritual assault and helping them resolve their spiritual conflicts. In Part Three we will explain how a Christ-centered home and your prayers as a parent can help shield your child from Satan's schemes. And in Chapter 13 we will outline the steps by which children of all ages can find freedom in Christ.

We strongly recommend that you read *The Bondage Breaker* (Harvest House) and its companion, *Victory Over the Darkness* (Regal Books), in conjunction with this study. They will help you realize the power of your identity and freedom in Christ so you can better help your child resist the enemy's seduction.

Finally, Steve and I want to offer you our hope. We are not without battle scars of our own from resisting the evil one. We have actively pursued our own freedom in Christ and have worked with thousands of adults and children who have been deceived by the father of lies. This is a winnable war, and it is a war we must win for the sake of our kids and the cause of Christ.

PART 1

xxxxxxxxxxxxxxxxxxxxxxxxxxxxxxxxxxxxxxxxxxxxxxxxxxxxxxxxxxxxxxxxxxxxxxxxxxxxxx

The Seductive World

xxxxxxxxxxxxxxxxxxxxxxxxxxxxxxxxxxxxxxxxxxxxxxxxxxxxxxxxxxxxxxxxxxxxxxxxxxxxxx

Chapter 1

SOMETHING WICKED THIS WAY COMES

xxxxxxxxxxxxxxxxxxxxxxxxxxxxxxxxxxxxxxxxxxxxxxxxxxxxxxxxxxxxxxxxxxxx

Two boys, Will and Jim, live in a small town in Illinois in the 1930s. One October, Dark's Pandemonium Carnival comes to town, much to the delight and excitement of the entire community, especially the two boys. Will and Jim are enchanted by the rides and shows and charmed by the handsome and mysterious Mr. Dark.

In their fascination, the boys sneak into the carnival after hours. To their horror they discover that the carnival is not what it appears. Townspeople who are lured to the carnival by its glitter and magic are secretly being captured, mesmerized, and turned into sideshow freaks.

The two boys are discovered and pursued by evil spirits, terrifying dreams of tarantulas, and the sinister Mr. Dark himself. Dark finally catches the boys and drags them back to the carnival to do away with them. Only the unlikely heroics of Will's father, the town's spineless librarian, and a fortuitous thunder and lightning storm foil Mr. Dark's scheme. The entire carnival is vacuumed up by a tornado-like cloud and disappears.

This story, *Something Wicked This Way Comes*, is from the imagination of science fiction writer Ray Bradbury. It appeared first as a book and then as a movie. In his tale of two boys caught in the classic struggle between good and evil, Bradbury displays uncanny insight into Satan's devious and relentless seduction of our children. For example:

> Mr. Dark appears to offer the boys happiness and fun, but his real intent is their destruction. The Bible says, "Satan disguises himself as an angel of light" (2 Corinthians 11:14), but his purpose is "to steal, and kill, and destroy" (John 10:10). Satan is out to destroy our children.
>
> Mr. Dark's carnival is called Pandemonium. In John Milton's classic, *Paradise Lost*, Pandemonium was the name given to the capital of Hell, the abode of the demons (notice that "demon" is right in the middle of the word). Satan is assisted in his seductive schemes by "the spiritual forces of wickedness in the heavenly places" (Ephesians 6:12).
>
> The only thing Mr. Dark fears is the storm, because the lightning illuminates his dark corners and the rain washes away his dust. The only way to dispel the darkness of Satan's seduction is to walk in the light ourselves and teach our children to do the same (1 John 1:5-7).
>
> Will's father, who has a history of cowardice, is the hero who races to the carnival in the nick of time to rescue Will and his friend Jim. Similarly, you as a parent may not feel fully qualified, but God desires to use you to guard your children from spiritual seduction as you "bring them up in the discipline and instruction of the Lord" (Ephesians 6:4).

The seduction of our children is no fairy tale or science fiction story. There is a real battle going on for our kids' minds. And the two major fronts of this battle center on two essential realities that, if not understood, will lead to the disintegration of the Christian family and confusion in the church of Christ. In this chapter we will explore these two realities and Satan's attempt to discredit them in the lives of our children.

Who Do You Think You Are?

The first essential reality relates to the believer's identity in Christ. If our children don't understand their worth in Christ, the enemy will try to convince them that they are worthless. And when a child thinks he's worthless he will behave as if he's worthless, bringing destruction to himself and to his family, as the following letter illustrates.

Dear Neil,

I was born to the two meanest people I have ever met in my life! I remember as a three-year-old my mom locked my dad out of the house, and him asking me to open the door. My next memory was of dad asking if he could at least have my younger sister. I can still recall the pain when I realized that Dad didn't want me. The voices probably started then: "You're so worthless that your father doesn't even want you."

My mother was so bitter and mean that I feared for my life. I would not eat any food unless she ate first, because I was afraid she would poison me. On top of that, my uncle molested me over a three-year period.

My image of God was like Mom and Dad. He was sitting up there ready to smash me for any small infraction. I never remember feeling loved. Every message I got from my family was negative. The inner voices kept reminding me, "You're ugly, you're disgusting, you're unworthy, God couldn't possibly love you."

I was in a codependency group for children of dysfunctional families when I was invited to your video series, "Resolving Personal and Spiritual Conflicts." Through your ministry I have found the answer: Jesus Christ. Now I know that the real battle is for my mind. Since I learned how to pray the depression is gone, the voices are gone, and the evil thing that has been in my room for the past 10 years is gone. I have peace within for the first time in my life.

There are countless numbers of kids growing up believing that they are no good and that God doesn't love them. They have never been fortified with the truth of who they are in Christ. They have never been taught that there is an accuser of the brethren (Revelation 12:10) or that Satan erects strongholds in their minds against a true knowledge of God (2 Corinthians 10:5). In their ignorance the enemy delights in convincing them that they are something they're not.

Sinner or Saint?

Our kids are growing up with an identity crisis because we aren't sharing the whole gospel with them. The church has primarily presented Christ as the Savior who died for our sins. We are challenged to believe in Him so we can go to heaven when we die. This is a marvelous truth, but it's only half the gospel.

The real issue of the gospel is that we *were* dead in our trespasses and sins but have *now* received eternal life in Christ (Ephesians 2:1; John 3:36). Jesus went to the cross to die for our sins. He cured the disease that caused us to die spiritually (Romans 6:23). Then He was resurrected in order that we may have life (John 11:25,26). As Christians, eternal life isn't something we get when we die; we have it now. We're no longer hell-bound sinners; we're heaven-bound saints.

But we have confused ourselves and our children by calling ourselves "sinners saved by grace" when the Bible calls us saints who occasionally sin. The difference is profound. If your child still thinks he's a sinner, he will easily be convinced to do what sinners do: sin. Rather, every born-again child of God is a saint who has been transferred out of the domain of darkness into the kingdom of Christ (Colossians 1:13). The more your child believes that he is a saint because of his faith in Christ's death and resurrection, the more he will live like a saint.

Every believer, even the smallest child who has trusted Christ as Savior, is dead to sin and spiritually alive in Christ right now. This reality is the basis for our identity; we are saints. Many Christians, not realizing who they are in Christ, take their identity from what they do. They sin, so they think they're sinners. But it's not what we do that determines who we are; it's who we are that determines what we do. If your child believes he is a sinner, Satan will have little difficulty encouraging him to sin. But if he believes he is a spiritually alive saint in Christ, he will begin to live like one, even though he will occasionally sin.

Your most important task as a parent is to lead your child to Christ. But don't stop there. You must continue to help him understand his true identity and realize his spiritual heritage as a child of God. If you don't teach him who he is in Christ, our wicked enemy will surely convince him otherwise.

Lies, Lies, Lies

Satan's greatest weapons for confusing our kids in relation to their identity are his lies. He is the father of lies (John 8:44), and he works undercover. His primary activity is covert, not overt. He takes advantage of children whose parents are not protecting their minds against his fiery darts with the belt of truth and the shield of faith (Ephesians 6:11-17). Silently the battle goes on for their minds. If you don't tell them they have no way of knowing that the thoughts they are thinking are really subtle lies from Satan himself.

Can Christians be tricked into acting on Satan's lies? Think about it. Did King David know that it was Satan who moved him to take a census in Israel (1 Chronicles 21:1ff)? If he did would he knowingly obey Satan? Did Judas Iscariot know that it was the devil who put into his heart the plan to betray Jesus (John 13:2)? If it was Judas' idea, why did he hang himself afterward? And was it Ananias' idea to lie to the Holy Spirit about the price of the land he sold (Acts 5:3)? If so, why did Peter attribute the lie to Satan?

If these men had known that Satan was behind the ideas in their heads, would they have followed through with them? I doubt it. Nor would your child follow through with his evil thoughts if he knew where they were coming from. What they are up against is mega-deception. For example, if we tempted your child to do something wrong, he would know it. If we accused him, he would know it. But if we deceived him, he wouldn't know it. Satan is in the deceiving business. He is sneaky, wily, sly, crafty, and cunning.

He is out to trick, trap, cheat, delude, and outwit your child any way he can. He intends to fill your child's mind with confusion, doubt, discouragement, disbelief, and despair, and to do so without being suspected or detected.

God has forewarned us: "The Spirit clearly says that in later times some will abandon the faith and follow deceiving spirits and things taught by demons" (1 Timothy 4:1 NIV). God knows that if Satan can get us to believe a lie, he can control our lives.

That's why the discipline for Ananias in the early church—instant death—was so severe. Sex and drugs bring bondage, but the lies of Satan are keeping far more people from experiencing the freedom that Christ purchased for them. That's why Jesus prayed, "I do not ask Thee to take them out of the world, but to keep them from the evil one.... Sanctify them in the truth; Thy word is truth" (John 17:15,17). That's why the first piece of spiritual armor we are commanded to put on is the "belt of truth" (Ephesians 6:14 NIV). It is truth that sets us free (John 8:32). We must teach our kids the truth about their identity in Christ or they will fall for Satan's lies.

Many Christians feel defeated and reason that they lack the power they need to resist Satan. So they pursue power by seeking religious experiences and chasing after "anointed" teachers. But we already have the power; we just don't see it. That's why Paul wrote, "I pray that the eyes of your heart may be enlightened, so that you may know what is the hope of His calling, what are the riches of the glory of His inheritance in the saints [not sinners!], and what is the surpassing greatness of His power toward us who believe" (Ephesians 1:18,19).

The power of the devil is in the lie, but the power of the Christian is in the truth. Replace the lie with the truth and Satan's power is broken. We're going to do our best in this book to expose the seductive lies of Satan which are rampant in our culture, in the media, and in secular education. But you'll never win the battle just by picketing New Age bookstores or burning all the Ouija boards in your community. Your best defense against Satan's lies is to submerge yourself and your children in God's truth. You may not be able to change much of the external world, but you can win the battle for the mind of your child by embracing the truth.

WHERE IN THE WORLD IS THE DEVIL?

The second essential reality that Satan would like to discredit in our culture is the existence of the spiritual world. The devil is alive and operating in our world, but he has disguised his operation as something like Mr. Dark's carnival: intriguing, harmless fun. The fact that he is enjoying some success is evident all around us. Movies like *Ghostbusters, Ghost, Poltergeist,* and *Field of Dreams* glorify experiences with spirits. Psychics and channelers are frequent guests on talk shows. New Age philosophy is being modeled in Saturday morning cartoons. And on Halloween we dress up our children as witches, goblins, slashers, and monsters. Meanwhile, behind the scenes, Satan is systematically destroying the fabric of our society because he has convinced us that he's just a harmless little man in a red suit carrying a pitchfork.

The effect of this delusion can be devastating to our kids. For example, if your child experiences a dark presence in his room some night (and most kids do), he won't want to tell about it because he may be afraid he's losing touch with reality. Or if he struggles with negative thoughts (and most kids do) or inner voices, he will think he's going crazy. If Satan can convince your child that the devil and demons are just cartoon characters, your child will assume the guilt and the blame for the enemy's work.

A Person, Not a Force

The facts about the spiritual world are clearly stated by Paul: "Our struggle is not against flesh and blood, but against the rulers, against the powers, against the world forces of this darkness, against the spiritual forces of wickedness in the heavenly places (Ephesians 6:12). The concept of Satan was not manufactured in the twentieth century. Orthodox Christianity has always held the belief in a personal devil (not just an impersonal evil force). C.S. Lewis wrote: "There is no neutral ground in the universe: every square inch, every split second, is claimed by God and counterclaimed by Satan."[1] Alert your child that a very real devil is intent on spoiling his life. But also assure him that in Christ he has the authority to defeat Satan's schemes.

During a conference, I noticed a lady who wouldn't sing with the rest of the group and seemed quite agitated. She slipped me a note after a morning session: "Please don't leave town without helping me. I have been diagnosed as having multiple personalities and a disassociative disorder."

During our time together the Lord revealed that when she was seven years old a terrifying dark presence appeared in her room. It told her it would kill her unless she granted its request to share her body. The presence didn't leave until the day we met together. Later she wrote:

> Before I met with you, I lived mostly in a very tiny corner of my mind. Even then I could never escape the

commanding voices, the filthy language, or the accusing anger. So I tried to separate myself from my mind altogether and live a disassociated life from it.

I started hearing voices and having imaginary friends when I was seven years old. Bulimia began at age 10, promiscuity at age 12. I spent 10 years in a cult. When I came out of the cult, I sought deliverance at the suggestion of a Catholic priest. But I beat up the priest and left bruised myself. It frightened me so badly I never did anything about it again.

I became a Christian in 1979 and struggled continually to believe that God actually accepted me, wanted me, and cared for me. I could never hear God's still, small voice in my mind without being punished for it by the other voice.

When that presence started to manifest in your office I was so afraid we would both be beaten up. With confident direction it went away without any commotion or injury to anyone.

I am now of a sound mind; the voices are gone. I feel clean and fresh inside for the first time I can remember. I don't live in a tiny corner of my mind or outside my body. I live inside now with my Lord. What a profound difference! There are no words to adequately describe the peacefulness and the absence of pain and torment that I now experience daily.

I wish that this woman's experience of childhood seduction was an exception. But I have counseled hundreds of adults who can trace their problems back to childhood. That's why it is critical that you teach your children the reality of the spiritual world and equip them to defeat Satan's attempts to seduce them with his lies.

Voices in the Darkness

The concept of hearing voices is openly espoused in the secular media. The main character in the popular movie *Field of Dreams* hears an inner voice while standing in his cornfield at night. It's loud, direct, and very spooky! At first he's a little freaked out by the voice, but he is intrigued enough to test the voice's advice. It leads to a grand adventure that culminates in meeting the ghost of his deceased father, forgiving him, and saving the family farm from foreclosure. Was the movie just an entertaining fantasy, or is Satan subtly promoting in our culture nice little spirit guides that will resolve all our problems?

According to brain-mind researcher Willis Harmon, many people hear voices, but few are willing to admit it to anyone but their closest friends. "It's just one of those things we don't talk about," said the president of the Institute of Noetic Sciences in Sausalito, California. "I've talked to businessmen, scientists, educators, well-educated professional people, and not only is it reasonably common, it's cherished. It's invited."[2]

Mental Illness or Spiritual Bondage?

New Age proponents like Harmon are trying to give credibility to a phenomenon that was once understood as mental illness. Psychiatrists prescribe antipsychotic drugs for schizophrenics and others who admit that they hear voices. A common bit of advice among recovering alcoholics is, "Don't pay attention to the committee in your head." People seldom share the mental struggle going on inside them for fear that people will think they are going crazy. But I have counseled hundreds who were hearing voices, and every one of the voices was demonic. Your children need to know that inner voices are the suggestions of a real devil that must be countered and dispelled by the truth.

In the Western world demonization is seldom considered as a possible cause of mental illness. Experts define mental health as "being in touch with reality and relatively free of anxiety." From the world's perspective, anybody under spiritual attack would fail on both counts. If your child reports hearing voices or sensing a dark presence in his room, most counselors will consider him neurotic or psychotic because his experience is out of touch with reality.

From a biblical view, the one out of touch with reality is the counselor who disavows the reality of the spiritual world. Mental health for the Christian is having a true knowledge of God and of our identity as His children. If our kids really knew that God loved them, that He would never leave or forsake them, that their sins are forgiven, that they will live forever with all their needs provided for, would they be mentally healthy? Absolutely.

Conversely, the greatest determinant of mental illness is a false concept of God and who we are. Visit a mental hospital and you will see some of the most religious people you've ever met. But their concept of God is distorted, and they have incredible delusions concerning their identity. Training your children in the truth is the best way to assure their spiritual and mental health.

I was conducting a conference for the leadership of one of America's flagship churches. The pastor is one of the most gifted Bible teachers I know, and his staff is among the best. I asked the 165 leaders present if they had ever experienced a direct encounter with something they knew was demonic such as a frightening presence in their room or an evil voice in their mind. Ninety-five percent answered yes. I went one step further to ask how many had been frightened by something pressing on them that they couldn't immediately respond to physically. At least a third raised their hand. Are these Christian leaders mentally ill? No, and neither are your children when they struggle against demonic influences in their lives.

Be Wary but Not Afraid

We warn our children about strangers in the streets. Don't you think we should warn them about "strangers" in their rooms? Our research suggests that 50 percent of Christian kids have encountered an evil presence in their rooms. Most of my students at seminary have had such an experience, and by the time they complete my class on resolving spiritual conflicts, several tell about having such an experience that semester. Would you know what to do if your child was terrorized by a presence in his room? Do you fear such a possibility?

Most people fear demonic things they can't see, but have no fear of God. That's just the opposite of what Scripture commands. We are told to fear the Lord (Proverbs 1:7), but we are never told to fear Satan. Fear of the devil is an inappropriate response to the reality of the spiritual world. Knowing his schemes and learning to resist him and take authority over him is the biblical response. God promises: "In the fear of the Lord there is strong confidence, and his children will have refuge" (Proverbs 14:26).

Fear is a major strategy of Satan to keep your children in bondage. I counseled a pastor's daughter who was sexually molested by a neighbor when she was quite young. The experience left her psychologically scarred and in spiritual bondage. She captured the fear element in a poem she wrote:

STOP! Don't look now. Don't even turn around!
    Something or someone is following you.
Hear its footsteps? No! But its presence is felt.
    Slowing down will only bring it closer.
So keep running ahead. Run as fast as you can!

How does it feel trying to escape what is there
    but can't be heard,
realizing that if you turn to face its frightening
    truth, it may strike you down
and leave you a ragged heap of self-pity
    helplessly laying on the ground?

So keep on running, and don't ever stop.
    Even though every step that is taken makes it
        bigger!
    Every mile run makes it harder to turn around.
The farther you run the harder you will fall.
    Finally you stumble or run out of breath.

There you lie,
    crumpled, broken, maybe even dead,
because you failed to turn around and face the
    truth,
    face the inevitable.

When you finally realized its presence you
    remembered, and it scared you.
It was no longer a small, silent stranger but a
    giant!
Now you no longer ignore it.
    It is worshipped. Because it is feared!

When the Lord released her from the spiritual bondage, the fear was gone, replaced by peace. She later wrote me this note: "When I looked in the mirror, I saw a woman I had never seen before. It was not the face of the ugly distorted creature reflected before. The first thought that crossed my mind was, 'I am my father's daughter, a clean and pure vessel.'"

Spiritual, Psychological, or Neurological?

The most common question I hear from parents who believe the Bible and accept the reality of the spiritual world is, "When is a child's problem spiritual and when is it psychological or neurological?" Your child's problems are always psychological. His mind, will, and emotions, along with developmental issues, always contribute something to the problem and are necessary for the resolution. At the same time, his problems are always spiritual. God is always present, and your child is always needful of Him. Furthermore, it is never safe for your child to take off the armor of God. The possibility of his being deceived, tempted, and accused by Satan is a continuous reality.

Our culture assumes that any problem related to the mind must be psychological or neurological. Why can it not be spiritual? We must take into account the total realm of reality: body, soul, and spirit. If we don't we will polarize into a psychotherapeutic ministry that ignores spiritual reality or some kind of deliverance ministry that ignores developmental issues or human responsibility. I have assured hundreds of people under spiritual attack that they are not going crazy but that there is a battle going on for their minds. The relief this insight brings to people is incredible.

I fully acknowledge that some child-behavior problems are caused by chemical imbalances or glandular disorders. For these you had better see your family physician. But it seems that the last possibility to be considered is always the spiritual, and only after every other possible natural explanation has been exhausted. But since we are instructed to seek first the kingdom of God (Matthew 6:33), why not check out the spiritual area first? Frankly, I approach every problem hoping it *is* spiritual in nature, because I know on the authority of the Word of God that the problem is resolvable. If the battle is for the mind, we can win that war.

Many parents react in horror at the suggestion that their child could have a demonic problem. "Can't be," they respond. "I'm a Christian and so is my child." Being a Christian doesn't provide blanket protection from the god of this world. If it did, why are we admonished to put on the armor of God, to take every thought captive in obedience to Christ, to resist the devil, to stand firm, and to be alert and sober, for the devil is roaring like a hungry lion seeking someone to devour? What will happen if we don't do these things? I have seen what happens in the lives of Christian children who were in bondage because a parent wasn't spiritually responsible and opened a door of opportunity for Satan.

We need a safe way to check out the spiritual realm without traumatizing the child. In my book *The Bondage Breaker*, I delineated the steps to freedom in Christ that take into account the whole person. These steps have been modified for use with children in Part Three of this book.

In Ray Bradbury's story, the Pandemonium Carnival featured a number of tempting activities and attractions that were designed to lure young Will and Jim into Mr. Dark's evil web. Similarly, Satan has surrounded your child with a world full of subtle influences designed to seduce and trap him. In the next several chapters we will explore many of those influences.

Chapter 2

DABBLING IN
THE DARKNESS

xxxxxxxxxxxxxxxxxxxxxxxxxxxxxxxxxxxxxxxxxxxxxxxxx

J oyce, a graduate student, had been in counseling for years. When she attended one of my conferences she was confronted with the need to forgive her mother, something she had been trying to do through counseling without success. But during the conference something clicked, and Joyce was able forgive her mother from her heart.

Joyce felt her burden lift as she drifted off to sleep one night. Then she was awakened by a horrible nightmare similar to others that had plagued her since childhood. She wrote to me explaining how God used the experience to help her understand the origin of her unforgiveness and other problems:

> Neil, as a child I religiously watched "Bewitched," my favorite TV show. This show sparked my interest in spiritual powers. I read books on ghosts, ESP, palm reading, and even spells and curses. I also played with a magic eight ball, Ouija board, and magic set. I knew that there was evil power in the world, and I wanted that power to get back at my mom for the way she treated me.

I clearly recall my first nightmare in the third grade. In it I met the devil, and he put a curse on me. I tried to use my dolls for voodoo on my mother, and I considered putting a curse on her. By the sixth grade I was reading Edgar Allan Poe. It was the only thing I craved. I was so depressed I even became suicidal.

By God's grace I was saved soon after that. But I have struggled as a Christian with issues like forgiving my mom. After your conference I realized that my childhood fascination with evil was at the root of my difficulties. I have since renounced my previous involvement with the occult and have dealt with all the lies I have been living with for years. I am finally free!

My conferences are full of good Christian people like Joyce who struggle with victory in their daily lives because they dabbled in the occult during childhood. They may have done so innocently out of curiosity or purposely as Joyce did in retaliation for difficult family relationships. No matter how people get into the dark side, Satan takes advantage of the opportunity and establishes strongholds in their lives. Hundreds of people attending my conferences walk free from bondages that have harassed them for years when they renounce the occultic practices they were involved in as children.

But our exposure to the kingdom of darkness as children is elementary compared to the onslaught confronting our kids in the last years of the twentieth century. With the rise of the New Age movement, the popularity of occultic practices and trinkets, and the growing acceptance of Satanism, demonic influence is spreading among our children like wildfire.

OUR KIDS ARE PLAYING WITH FIRE

How prevalent is this intrusion of the powers of darkness among our children? Steve and I developed a survey in hopes of finding out. We questioned 286 students in one Christian high school and tabulated these startling responses:

> Forty-five percent said they have experienced a "presence" (seen or heard) in their room that scared them.
>
> Fifty-nine percent said they've harbored bad thoughts about God.
>
> Forty-three percent said they find it mentally hard to pray and read their Bible.
>
> Sixty-nine percent reported hearing "voices" in their head, like there was a subconscious voice talking to them.
>
> Twenty-two percent said they frequently entertain thoughts of suicide.
>
> Seventy-four percent think they are different than others ("It works for others but not for me").

The school administration was obviously concerned about these results and started asking students about their experiences. They found out that nearly every student in the school had played "Bloody Mary," a popular party game among some groups of kids. A common version of the game requires a child to go into a completely darkened bathroom alone, spin around six times, face the mirror, and call upon Bloody Mary to show herself. In many cases these children saw something frightening in the mirror. There was no physical explanation for seeing anything in a totally dark room. These kids had unwittingly opened themselves up to demonic powers. School leaders discovered other seemingly harmless activities among the students that contributed to the problems revealed in the survey.

Bloody Mary is only one of the "innocent" ways our children are giving Satan a foothold in their lives. Games like the Ouija board and Dungeons and Dragons are other common means by which kids are introduced to the occult. The music, movies, magazines, television programs, and substances our children are exposed to create gaping doors of opportunity for Satan to seduce them. At one public high school in Southern California, 133 students were referred to the school psychologist during the first six weeks of classes because of their involvement with Satanism and the occult. Most kids don't even realize the spiritual bondage they are submitting to when participating in these activities. What's worse, most parents don't either.

Our survey at the Christian school prompted us to broaden our research. We surveyed 1725 students (433 junior high and 1292 senior high) attending Christian schools and camps. The first eight questions on the survey dealt with experiences that are common among people under demonic attack. Question 9 asked students to indicate if they had participated in certain occultic practices. The figures indicate the percentage of students who answered "yes" to each question:

Question	Junior High Yes	Senior High Yes
1. Have you ever experienced a presence in your room (seen or heard) that scared you?	50%	47%

Question	Juniors Yes	Seniors Yes
2. Do you struggle with bad thoughts about God?	44%	54%
3. Is it mentally hard for you to pray and read your Bible?	25%	37%
4. Have you heard "voices" in your head like there was a subconscious self talking to you, or have you struggled with really bad thoughts?	57%	70%
5. Have you frequently had thoughts of suicide?	12%	20%
6. Have you ever had impulsive thoughts to kill someone, like, "Grab that knife and kill that person"?	21%	24%
7. Have you ever thought you were different than others (it works for others but not for you)?	73%	71%
8. Do you like yourself?	89%	82%
9. Have you ever been involved with:		
astral projection?	2%	2%
table lifting?	8%	8%
fortune telling?	8%	10%
astrology?	11%	20%
Dungeon and Dragons?	18%	16%
crystals or pyramids?	5%	3%
Ouija boards?	15%	26%
automatic writing?	1%	2%
tarot cards?	3%	6%
palm reading?	7%	12%
spirit guides?	1%	2%
blood pacts?	3%	6%

Among the 1725 students surveyed were 864 students who checked "no" on all inquiries regarding occult experiences (Question 9). But notice that even without a background of dabbling in the dark areas listed these 864 students reported an alarmingly high incidence of mental seduction:

Question	Yes
1. Have you ever experienced a presence in your room (seen or heard) that scared you?	40%
2. Do you struggle with bad thoughts about God?	43%
3. Is it mentally hard for you to pray and read your Bible?	31%
4. Have you heard "voices" in your head like there was a subconscious self talking to you, or have you struggled with really bad thoughts?	58%
5. Have you frequently had thoughts of suicide?	14%
6. Have you ever had impulsive thoughts to kill someone, like, "Grab that knife and kill that person"?	16%
7. Have you ever thought you were different than others (it works for others but not for you)?	67%

There are several reasons why kids who don't play around with occultic practices are still susceptible to demonic oppression and seduction.

The first is unforgiveness. Satan's greatest avenue of access to all Christians—young and old—is unforgiveness. Paul urges us to forgive one another "in order that no advantage be taken of us by Satan; for we are not ignorant of his schemes" (2 Corinthians 2:10,11). Whether a child plays with a Ouija board or believes in horoscopes or not, if he harbors an attitude of unforgiveness toward someone, he makes himself an easy target for Satan's schemes. From my experience in counseling, 95 percent of the people who harbor unforgiveness admit that their parents are at the top of the list. Your child may be vulnerable to demonic attack because he or she has not forgiven you for a real or perceived offense.

The second major source of demonic seduction is the iniquity of the parents passed on to the next generation. Parents who ignore God and His law pass their sin and its effects on to their children, great-grandchildren, and great-great-grandchildren (Exodus 20:5,6; 34:6,7). A woman attending one of my conferences told me about her 11-year-old daughter, Charla. In addition to struggling with depression and interpersonal problems, Charla exhibited lesbian behavior. When Charla's mother told me that her husband was verbally abusive and unsupportive in the family, I sensed that Charla's problem might be spiritual because of her father's influence, something her mother had never once considered.

After the conference she asked Charla if she had ever heard voices in her head. Realizing that her mother was willing to accept what she was experiencing, Charla readily shared the growing nightmare within. She said that four distinct personalities had been talking to her. One demonic voice seemed to respond to her anger (see Ephesians 4:25-27 to see the biblical connection), promising her power to read minds and to put thoughts into other people's minds if she would worship him.

Shortly afterward Charla was led through the steps to freedom we will discuss in Part Three. Charla's mother can hardly believe the difference in her little girl.

Another avenue of seduction that is not directly related to the occult is the extensive realm of worldly amusements and distractions. In Chapters 5 and 6 we will explore in detail how elements such as certain fashions, music, movies, and drugs contribute to the seduction of our children.

DOORWAYS INTO THE DARK

We further analyzed the survey responses to determine if the kids who dabbled in occult experiences were even more susceptible to demonic influence than those who indicated no such experiences. We compared the 864 students claiming no involvement in the occult with students who have dabbled in each of the 12 activities on the survey. The eye-opening results are revealed in Figure 2a.

Notice that the students admitting involvement in each of the 12 activities registered a higher percentage of yes answers to the first seven questions than the 864 students reporting no involvement. And for Question 8, "Do you like yourself?", those dabbling in the darkness generally registered a lower percentage of yes answers than the uninvolved group. In some cases the difference between the groups is dramatic. For example, thoughts of suicide and impulsive thoughts to kill are significantly more apparent among students having experiences in the occult.

Please understand that these responses are the results of a simple survey, not a carefully controlled scientific study. The results in no way establish causation. It is very important to realize that the occultic experiences mentioned are not the sole explanation for the problems the students are having. But you should be convinced by these responses, as we are, that if your kids dabble in these activities they are opening a doorway to the darkness they will later regret.

Just what are the problems with the occult activities listed on the survey? The following explanations should

	Presence in Room?	Bad thoughts about God?	Hard to pray or read Bible?	Heard "voices" or bad thoughts?	Thoughts of suicide?	Impulsive thoughts to kill?	Thought you were different?	Do you like yourself?
No Involvement.....864	40%	43%	31%	58%	14%	16%	67%	86%
Astral Projection 44	68%	72%	50%	79%	36%	29%	86%	78%
Table Lifting..........149	61%	63%	48%	82%	30%	28%	73%	74%
Fortune Telling......180	63%	69%	43%	83%	29%	35%	82%	77%
Astrology...............321	57%	63%	39%	80%	28%	31%	79%	75%
Dungeons and Dragons 286	56%	66%	40%	77%	22%	43%	79%	87%
Crystals or Pyramids..............72	72%	73%	51%	77%	36%	37%	77%	80%
Ouija Board 416	58%	62%	37%	76%	27%	35%	76%	75%
Automatic Writing.....................35	71%	54%	51%	85%	37%	37%	85%	37%
Tarot Cards..............99	66%	70%	43%	84%	44%	46%	78%	69%
Palm Reading 192	60%	67%	45%	81%	35%	43%	77%	74%
Spirit Guides 37	72%	72%	45%	89%	48%	51%	81%	68%
Blood Pacts 100	68%	67%	53%	82%	36%	49%	81%	74%

Figure 2a: Student occult involvement comparison.

help you understand why you and your children should stay away from any involvement with these activities.

Astral projection supposedly describes an out-of-body travel experience. Occultists define it as the conscious separation of the astral body from the physical body resulting in an altered state of consciousness and sometimes in different qualities of perception. In reality, astral projection is nothing more than a mind trip.

Your children need to know that Christians should not seek astral projection experiences. We will separate from our bodies only once for the purpose of being with the Lord (2 Corinthians 5:6-8). Anything else is a demonic counterfeit.

Table lifting has many variations. It's usually played as a party game in which kids try to lift an object with powers other than physical strength. Even though it is not intended to conjure up something evil, bad things often result because such activities are concerted efforts to tap into the supernatural.

Warn your children that deliberately trying to call upon supernatural powers apart from God is never good. It's the same thing Satan tempted Christ to do when he asked Him to use His supernatural powers independent of God the Father. If the "game" works, you can be sure that the power that appears is not God's.

Fortune telling is an attempt to predict the future through divination. All occultic practices claim to enable people to know the future or be able to read minds. The lure of knowledge and power is a powerful hook for the naive, and our children are especially vulnerable to it.

Satan doesn't have perfect knowledge of the future, nor does he know what a believer is thinking. But he does know more than can be humanly explained. Alert your children that we are not to consult mediums or spiritists (Leviticus 19:31; 20:6; 20:27). We are to trust God for tomorrow and live responsible lives today.

Astrology is a system based on the belief that celestial bodies influence human beings. Astrologers claim that an individual is affected by the cosmic array that existed in the heavens at the time of his birth. Each person was born under the influence of one of the 12 signs of the zodiac. Astrologers plot the heavens and read the "signs" (horoscope) for the purposes of gaining insight into a person's character and personality. Mundane astrology deals with large-scale phenomena (e.g., wars, natural disasters, political trends, and the destiny of nations). Horary astrology supposedly determines the implications of undertaking particular actions at certain times.

More people read their horoscope each day than read the Bible. Some say they read their horoscopes only for fun; they don't really believe them. That shows a pathetic misunderstanding of how the mind works. Suppose your child reads in his horoscope that he should beware of strangers today. He may laugh about it, but when he meets a stranger later in the day, guess what thought is still fresh in his mind? The fact that he didn't believe his horoscope didn't stop the power of suggestion from planting the idea in his mind. Educate your child that astrology is a counterfeit guidance system based on nothing more than chance. It should be avoided.

Dungeons and Dragons is a habit-forming fantasy game of death and the underworld. We will explain the game and its effects in greater detail in Chapter 5. But notice from the survey that 43 percent of the students who have played the game reported impulsive thoughts to kill as opposed to only 16 percent among students who haven't played the game. Your kids should stay away from such games.

Crystals or pyramids. Crystals are mystical symbols of the spirit because they are solid and tangible while also being transparent. Among many shaman groups, natural crystals are power objects. The word "pyramid" means "glorious light," from the Greek word *pyros* for fire. Crystals and pyramids are routinely associated with the New Age movement. If your child is playing with crystals or pyramids he is probably involved with other New Age practices.

Ouija boards. When the Ouija board works, the players have tapped into the demonic. It is clearly an attempt to seek guidance apart from God. It is disconcerting that 416 of the Christian kids we surveyed had been involved with Ouija boards at some time. Warn your children that the Ouija board is not a simple board game like Monopoly. It can usher them into the harmful world of evil spirits. We will say more about Ouija boards in Chapter 5.

Automatic writing is practiced by spiritual mediums. The medium enters a trance and writes down the impressions that come to mind. It is an obvious counterfeit of the prophetic voice of God. God works through the active minds of His people, but occultic practices require a passive state of the mind. The occult actually bypasses the mind and the personality of the person involved, and a different personality emerges. It is no small concern to us that 35 of the students we surveyed at Christian schools and camps had functioned as mediums for automatic writing. Your children should be warned to leave any gathering where automatic writing or other mediumistic practices are taking place.

Tarot cards come in a pack of 78 and are often regarded as the precursor of modern playing cards. Tarot cards are commonly used for divination (fortune telling and guidance). The cards are divided into the Major Arcana (22 cards) and the Minor Arcana (56 cards). The latter consists of four suits—wands, swords, cups, and pentacles—and approximate the four suits in the modern card deck. The Major Arcana has archetypal significance, and the cards are regarded by occultists as symbolic meditative pathways that can be correlated with the Kabbalistic "Tree of Life." No Christian should have anything to do with tarot cards or any other type of divination (Deuteronomy 18:10, 11).

Palm reading or palmistry is the study and interpretation of the palm of the hand for the purpose of divination. Distinguishing features of the palm include whorls and line patterns and the color and texture of the skin. People have their palms read because they want insight into themselves or the future.

God asks regarding such acts of divination: "Is it because there is no God in Israel that you are going to inquire of Baal-zebub?" (2 Kings 1:3); "And when they say to you, 'Consult the mediums and the spiritists who whisper and mutter,' should not a people consult their God? Should they consult the dead on behalf of the living? To the law and to the testimony! If they do not speak according to this word, it is because they have no dawn" (Isaiah 8:19,20). Your children must learn to ask God to search their hearts and trust Him for their future instead of turning to established practices of divination such as palm reading.

Spirit guides are nothing more than demonic voices. New Age conferences have meditative practices that enable people to acquire their own spirit guides. Some spirits come by the laying on of hands, others through guided imagery or a mediumistic trance. One young lady in a church claimed that spirit guides were helpful spirits. If you think they are, let me share another survey result. Kids who have entertained spirit guides are by far the most troubled group. Over 50 percent have had impulsive thoughts to kill someone!

Blood pacts. There isn't a more obvious counterfeit to Christianity than making a blood pact. We are united with Christ and with each other through the sacrifice of Jesus Christ. His shed blood is the only basis for Christian heritage and fellowship. Any other blood pact is a counterfeit of Christ's work.

Satanists commonly draw blood and drink it at their ceremonies. It is a counterfeit of Christian communion where we eat the flesh and drink the blood of Christ by faith. Blood pacts have taken on a romantic notion among kids who become blood brothers and sisters by pricking their fingers and mingling their blood. Whether it is a childish game or a serious ritual, it must be renounced. One hundred of the students surveyed have made blood pacts. Next to those with spirit guides, this group is in the most trouble.

The fact that a large majority of the students surveyed think they are different than others reflects Satan's assault on the believer's identity in Christ discussed in Chapter 1. Every Christian is a full-fledged child of God. No one is inferior. Even the apostle Peter needed a dramatic vision to learn the truth that God loves all His children equally: "I most certainly understand now that God is not one to show partiality" (Acts 10:34).

It's not just occult practices such as those listed above that are seducing our kids into the darkness. The New Age movement permeating our society and our public education system today is the source of many pitfalls. And so much of the world's attempt to amuse and entertain our children leads them into the darkness. In the next four chapters we will reveal some of these dangers.

As we continue to expose Satan's schemes, remember: No matter how many dark doorways beckon to your kids, Christ is the ultimate door to freedom. Your job is not to try to eliminate the darkness in your child's life; you are simply to turn on the light of truth. In a sense it doesn't really matter how the lie approaches your child. It may come from the television set, a New Age school teacher, or a demonic spirit in his room. In any event, you must help him dwell on "whatever is true" (Philippians 4:8). As you do, the light will overpower the darkness and the enemy's seduction will fail.

Chapter 3

GROWING UP IN
IN A NEW AGE

xxxxxxxxxxxxxxxxxxxxxxxxxxxxxxxxxxxxxxxxxxxxxxxxxxxxxx

While speaking at a conference in Arizona, I (Steve) decided to take a quick afternoon trip to Sedona—a known center for the New Age movement—to gather first-hand information for this chapter. As I drove through town I saw New Age symbols and bookstores everywhere. But I also noticed several evangelical churches. I wondered how local pastors had responded to the challenge of ministering among New Agers.

After several attempts I found a pastor in his office. The church was directly next door to two New Age bookstores. After introducing myself I asked, "What's it like to pastor a church in a New Age center like Sedona?"

He looked bewildered. "I don't know what you're talking about," he said. "There really isn't a problem here. After all, not everyone living here is involved in the New Age."

I decided to rephrase my question. "With Sedona being a hot spot for New Age activity, what challenges have you faced trying to minister in this city?"

His response shocked me. "Young man, I learned a valuable lesson when I began my ministry. If you don't go looking for trouble, you won't find it." And that was the end of our short conversation.

Unfortunately this pastor's head-in-the-sand cop-out is all too characteristic of the church today. Whether we like it or not, the New Age is part of our culture, and its influence is present in sociology, theology, physical sciences, medicine, anthropology, history, sports, literature, and the arts. In 1989 an estimated 60 million people in the world dabbled in New Age or occultic thinking.[1]

According to Russell Chandler, religion writer for the *Los Angeles Times*, the New Age movement is probably the most widespread, powerful phenomenon affecting our culture today. Some New Agers believe the movement has the potential to impact the world as did the Renaissance or the Protestant Reformation. They believe it will usher in a new order of peace, prosperity, and perfection.

That's what Satan would love us to think. In reality, the New Age movement is simply opening the doors to his destructive influence in our culture even wider than before. Your kids are growing up in a world where occultic and satanic teachings and practices are condoned and even accepted as a normal part of everyday life. You must understand how the New Age is contributing to Satan's seduction of your children.

THE WIDE, WIDE WORLD
OF THE NEW AGE

The following figures reveal that satanic inroads into our culture are accompanying the spread of the New Age:

> Forty-five percent of all Americans believe that ghosts exist.

Thirty-one percent of all Americans believe that some people have magical powers.

Twenty-eight percent believe in witchcraft, 24 percent in black magic, and 20 percent in voodoo.[2]

Thirty-four million Americans are concerned with inner growth, including mysticism.

Forty-two percent of American adults believe they have been in contact with someone who has died.

Sixty-seven percent of American adults report having psychic experiences like extra-sensory perception (ESP).

Thirty million Americans—roughly one in four—now believe in reincarnation, a key tenet of the New Age.

Fourteen percent of Americans endorse the work of spirit mediums or trance channelers.

Sixty-seven percent of American adults read astrology reports (36 percent believe they are scientific).

A northern Illinois university survey found that more than half of Americans think extraterrestrial beings have visited earth (a belief held in many New Age circles).[3]

Going Public

It's amazing how New Age concepts have been introduced and popularized in the media. Entertainer and author Shirley MacLaine has turned the movement into a fad through her three bestselling New Age books and her TV miniseries, *Out on a Limb*. Celebrities like MacLaine publicly endorse their spirit guides on late night talk shows and offer recruitment challenges to viewers. Joyce De Witt, formerly of *Three's Company*, and Linda Evans, star of *Dynasty*, follow guidance from an imponderable entity named Mafu. Others publicly affirming their New Age connections include Wally "Famous" Amos, the chocolate chip cookie king, singers Helen Reddy and Tina Turner, actresses Marsha Mason and Lisa Bonet, and musician Paul Horn.[4]

New Age and occultic themes can be found in film epics like the *Star Wars* saga ("May the force be with you"), *The Exorcist* and *Cocoon* movies, *Angel Heart*, *Field of Dreams*, and *Ghost*, to name just a few. In the controversial film, *The Last Temptation of Christ*, pantheistic, mystic thinking is injected into the Christ figure who doubts his messiahship and struggles with lustful temptations.

New Age philosophy is being promoted publicly in many other ways. For example:

A leading New Age theoretician has lectured at the U.S. Army War College. The Army's Organizational Effectiveness School has used New Age-oriented curriculum in some of its programs.[5]

Major corporations hire New Age consultants to help increase employee productivity.

Our nation's courts are calling on psychics to use their reputed powers to weed out lying witnesses, pinpoint suspects, and locate missing bodies.[6]

There are New Age dating services, travel agencies, accountants, and even attorneys.

New Age products and gadgets flood the marketplace: singing Tibetan bowls, statues, crystals, pyramids, greeting cards, tarot cards, charms, pendants, fortune-telling devices, computer software, talismans, herbal medicines, "rebirthing" tanks, and colonic cleansers.

New Age books now occupy large sections in our major bookstores. In addition, *Time* magazine notes that there are more than 2,500 New Age or occultic bookstores in the U.S. alone. Sales of occult books, New Age books, and journals has turned into a billion-dollar-a-year business.[7]

Heavenly Appeal

On the surface the New Age movement appears to be very positive, supposedly meeting needs that organized Christianity has failed to meet. New Agers zealously seek an end to poverty, disease, homelessness, suffering, social discrimination, inequality, the destruction of the environment, and economic and political tyranny. They claim to have answers to the questions of life and boast in the ability to enable everyone to tap into his "hidden potential."

You may be thinking, "These are the right things to be concerned about. How can we find fault with these lofty goals?" The problem is not New Agers' goals but their source for reaching these goals. According to humanistic psychologist Maxine Negri, all human goals appear possible "not through Jesus Christ or Mohammed or other 'divine' messengers but through one's own human, independently earned spiritual enlightenment."[8] Shirley MacLaine stated at one of her "Connecting with a Higher Self" seminars, "We are at any given moment living the totality of everything. . . . Just remember that you are God and act accordingly."[9] The appeal of the New Age is being your own God, the aspiration that brought Satan into our world in the first place (Isaiah 14:12-14).

The New Age Is Old Hat

According to Russell Chandler, although new in style and vocabulary, the New Age movement is as old as Hinduism, Buddhism, Western occultism, and the mystical oracles of ancient Greece and Egypt. The New Age has simply rebuilt the theory of reincarnation into the language of Western humanistic psychology, science, and technology.[10] *Time* magazine calls the New Age "a combination of spirituality and superstition, fad and force, about which the only thing certain is that it is not new."[11]

The term "New Age" doesn't refer to any one group, collection of groups, or period in history. The New Age revival has historic ties to Sumerian, Indian, Egyptian, Chaldean, Babylonian, and Persian religious practices. For all practical purposes the present movement in the United States can be equated with the transplantation of Hindu philosophy through the Theosophical Society founded by Helena Blavatsky in the latter part of the nineteenth century. Madame Blavatsky, as she was known, promoted spiritism, seances, and basic Hindu philosophy while being distinctly antagonistic toward biblical Christianity.[12]

SIX PRINCIPLES OF
NEW AGE THINKING

According to Jeremy P. Tarcher, a spokesman for a Los Angeles firm that publishes New Age books, "No one speaks for the entire New Age community. Within the movement, there is no unanimity as to how to define it or even that it is significantly cohesive to be called a movement."[13]

But Tarcher and other New Age leaders would agree that the movement is based on certain premises. The following six principles of New Age form the "radical vision" shared by those involved in the movement. As you will see, each of these principles is a clever, subtle counterfeit of biblical Christianity. And since New Age is so pervasive in our society, your children are being impacted by these Satanically-inspired principles from the public school classroom to the television set in your family room. (A glossary of New Age terms is found in the Appendix.)

1. All is one, one is all. The New Age bottom line is the belief in monism. The entire universe swims in one great cosmic ocean. Every particle is part of one vast, interconnected process. There are no real differences between humans, animals, rocks, and even God. The differences are only apparent. All human ills stem from an inability to perceive reality's unity. For Christians, history is the story of mankind's fall into sin and restoration by God's saving grace. But for New Agers, history is humanity's fall into ignorance and gradual ascent into enlightenment.

Your child will be influenced to believe that creation is an undivided unity. Help him understand that creation is a diversity of beings and things created and sustained by God (Colossians 1:16,17). Satan would seduce your child to believe that he is divine in nature and that the real crisis he faces is ignorance, not evil. Teach your child that mankind is separate from God and lost because of his sin nature (Romans 3:10,23).

2. God is everything, everything is God. New Agers believe in pantheism, that everything in creation is part of God. Trees, snails, books, people, etc. are all one divine essence. A personal God is abandoned in favor of an impersonal energy force or consciousness. As researchers James Patterson and Peter Kim report, this New Age tenet is very popular in this country: "Americans seem to use God to refer to a general principle of good in life—or, sometimes, He (or She) is the creator who set off the Big Bang, but doesn't intervene in human affairs. For most Americans, God is not to be feared, or for that matter, loved."[14]

New Agers say, "We are all gods, so we might as well get good at it." That sounds just like what Satan said: "You will be like God" (Genesis 3:5). He knows that if God can be reduced from the almighty King and loving heavenly Father to a state humans can achieve, your child can be persuaded not to love Him or serve Him.

Pantheism is Satan's counterfeit for the one true God, the Father of our Lord Jesus Christ (Deuteronomy 6:4; Ephesians 1:3). The enemy would like your child to believe that "God" is not a person but an impersonal force resident in everything and everyone. Remind your child that God is a person, not an *it*, and that His personal attributes are detailed in the Bible (Exodus 3:6,14).

3. Self-realization. New Agers say, "Since we are gods, we need to know that we are gods. We must become cosmically conscious." The process of gaining the awareness of oneness with God is called at-one-ment, self-realization, God-realization, enlightenment, or attune-ment.

Jesus is regarded by the New Age as one of many "enlightened masters." He was such a dynamic person and teacher, they say, because He realized His essential Godness, something everyone is capable of doing. Two popular phrases in the movement are: "We too may share the Christ-consciousness" and "The savior out there is being replaced by the hero in here."

For New Agers, self-realization occurs through reincarnation. This theory states that the soul progresses through many life cycles according to the working out of one's karma. The final goal is to merge with God and end the painful birth-death-rebirth process. Some who reach this enlightened status claim to be "born-again."

Self-realization is Satan's counterfeit for biblical conversion. At-one-ment is a cheap imitation of Christ's atonement. Jesus is not just another enlightened master. He is the King of kings, the Lord of lords, and the Creator of the ages (Titus 2:13). Conversion is not a continuing experience of reincarnation or soul progression. Everyone lives once, dies once, and then faces the judgment (Hebrews 9:27). Salvation is a once-for-all experience of grace through faith (Ephesians 2:8,9).

4. A new world order. New Agers believe in a progressive, evolutionary harmonization and unification of world consciousness eventually reaching the "omega point" of a one-world government. A new global civilization and an eclectic world religion (some kind of Eastern mysticism, of course) is necessary because national boundaries are obsolete in a worldview where all is one. This unification of world consciousness will lead to world peace.

The "new world order" is Satan's counterfeit for the kingdom of God. Help your children understand that there can be no lasting harmony between people without a revolution in the human heart that only God's Spirit can effect through new birth (John 3:3). Total world peace and harmony will only be realized when God creates the new heaven and the new earth (Isaiah 65:17).

5. Reality is what you make it. New Agers claim that reality is determined by what they believe. By changing what they believe, they can change reality. There are no moral absolutes because there is no distinction between good and evil. Whatever you believe to be good is good, and whatever you believe to be evil is evil.

According to Patterson and Kim, the create-your-own-reality approach is catching on in a big way: "There is absolutely no moral consensus at all in the 1990s. Everyone is making up their own personal moral code—their own Ten Commandments. When we want to answer a question of right and wrong, we ask ourselves."[15]

One of the most prevalent examples of this line of thinking is seen in the teen sex crisis. Studies have shown that sexual activity among teenagers in the church is the same as among teens who don't attend church. Why are churchgoing teens so soft on sexual purity? Because they are picking up from the culture around them that there are no moral absolutes. Rather, they are being influenced to believe that they can do whatever makes them feel good or makes sense to them apart from any external authority, including God.

I was talking with a high school senior at a local restaurant one afternoon when he suddenly asked, "Steve, what do you think about sex before marriage? And don't give me any religious answers, 'cause I've already done it."

Here was a Christian boy who was looking for an opinion, not an authoritative response. I tossed his question back to him: "Kirk, what do *you* think about sex before marriage?"

"I think it's okay as long as you love each other and you're not hurting anyone," he responded. Kirk knew what the Bible says about premarital sex, but he preferred his own "reality," as do many Christian teens today.

Such is the influence of the New Age. Satan is substituting relative truth for God's truth. In New Age thinking, truth is perceived individually: "That's your truth, and this is my truth." But God's truth is absolute, and His moral law is clearly spelled out in His Word (John 8:32; 14:6). We must teach our children from infancy that God's Word endures forever (Psalm 117:2; 1 Peter 1:25).

6. *Holistic thinking.* New Agers call it the "paradigm shift." This shift is a distinctly new way of thinking about old problems: holistically, seeing everything as part of the pantheistic cosmos, instead of dualistically, with God and humanity being separate entities. Ultimately the shift can only take place through a mystical "awakening experience" that changes the way a person thinks, lives, communicates, and perceives reality. Once awakened, say New Agers, we will be able to deify humanity, deny death, and recognize that the real enemy is ignorance not evil. The New Age premise is that knowledge is the key to being awakened from our ignorance of our own divinity.

The paradigm shift to holistic thinking is a "lofty thing raised up against the knowledge of God" (2 Corinthians 10:5). Your child needs a new way of thinking, but it doesn't come about through a mystical awakening. God's version of new thinking only happens as we allow our minds to be renewed by Him (Romans 12:1,2).

Danger Ahead

Even the secular media is recognizing the potential danger of the New Age movement to our culture and our children. *Time* magazine stated: "The rise of the New Age is a barometer of the disintegration of American culture. Dostoyevsky said [that] anything is permissible if there is no God. But anything is also permissible if everything is God. . . . Once you've deified yourself, which is what the New Age is all about, there is no moral absolute. It's a recipe for ethical anarchy."[16] The insidious danger inherent in the movement is its view of the nature of reality, which admits to no absolutes. History has proven that relative standards of morality breed chaos and ultimately the fall of a society.

In 1922 Adolf Hitler began his national youth movement. He knew that if he could control the minds of the children he could control an entire generation. And by 1932 approximately 100,000 young people were part of Hitler's youth movement, and history records the appalling results of this madman's influence on those under his control.

This is the same strategy Satan has been using for centuries. The rise of the New Age movement is just another facet of his effort to seduce and control an entire generation. Let's rescue our kids by helping them prepare their minds for action (1 Peter 1:13). Remember: The New Age movement is deeply ingrained in every level of our society. We need to help our kids recognize Satan's subtle counterfeits and develop a Christ-centered, biblically-based perspective of life.

How can we accomplish this? Here are a few suggestions:

> Monitor what they watch and listen to from the entertainment world: movies, music, television shows, cartoons, etc. Be aware of the games they play and what they read for recreational purposes. Talk to them about how God's truth applies to the concepts being presented in the media. Help them understand

Satan's subtle attempts to seduce them through their recreation activities.

Take an active interest in their schoolwork and homework assignments. Be aware of what they are being taught. We will discuss the ways public education is being influenced by New Age and the occult in Chapter 4.

Encourage them in their personal relationship with Jesus Christ. Pray daily for their mental, physical, spiritual, and emotional well-being. Help them develop a lifestyle that pleases God and obeys His Word. Equip them to answer the great rationalization of our day, "Everybody's doing it; why shouldn't I? Everybody's breaking the rules; am I a complete fool to play by the rules myself?" Help them understand that they have the freedom to choose and that the best choice is to obey God.

Finally and most importantly, provide a positive, godly example of living by God's truth on a daily basis. Being a godly example doesn't require you to be perfect, but it does require that you be genuine and authentic in your faith. Are you an obedient, loving, forgiving Christian seven days a week or only on Sundays?

Being a good example involves allowing your kids to see how you handle failure as well as success. When you make a mistake or don't have all the answers, admit it. When you harm your child with a harsh attitude or word, apologize and ask his forgiveness. And be careful to practice what you preach.

One Wednesday night while serving as a youth pastor, I gave what I thought was an outstanding message to the youth group on the topic of building up one another. I challenged them to evaluate every word and action with the question, "Does this build up or edify?"

The following Saturday I was working with some students from the group during a church workday. We had just finished cleaning the hallway in the Sunday school building when two guys ran out of a classroom and carelessly spilled hundreds of tiny plastic beads all over the floor. "You dummies! Look at what you just did!" I barked.

The youth group responded in perfect unison, "Steve, does that build up or edify?" I suddenly realized that my example carried at least as much weight with them as my words.

It's little things like these that your kids will notice. If they see a gap between what you say and what you do, they will assume that a counterfeit lifestyle is the norm. But as they watch you recognize and dismiss Satan's counterfeits and embrace God's truth, they will learn to do the same.

Chapter 4

SEDUCTION IN
THE CLASSROOM

xxxxxxxxxxxxxxxxxxxxxxxxxxxxxxxxxxxxxxxxxxxxxxxxxxxxxxxxxxx

P ublic education has changed dramatically in the last two decades. We used to have three *R*'s, now we have four: reading, 'riting, 'rithmetic, and reproductive rights. Our schools have become battlefields for a wide array of causes and issues—school-based clinics, values clarification, evolution, self-esteem, and gay awareness. The dropout rate is increasing, and we are just waking up to the literacy problem. Kids are being alienated from their parents and traditional morality while being taught to rationalize rather than discern. We've certainly come a long way from the days of the little red schoolhouse.

The following is an excerpt from a paper entitled, "A Generation that Failed," which was presented at a conference on the state of American youth in 1988: "Imagine an American society where far too many people didn't come to work on time, where many who did were often spaced out on drugs and alcohol, where adults could not communicate intelligently and in writing with each other, where women with young children at home had no way to provide adequate care, and where adults and children lived in fear of random crime and violence."[1]

The conference went on to suggest that such a society was a distinct possibility in light of the current state of American youth. We have become a nation at risk because of the moral, spiritual, social, and intellectual decline of our young people. Much of this decline can be traced to the changes in public education concurrent with the expulsion of biblical values and the growing acceptance of New Age and occultic thinking and practices. And we are just seeing the tip of the iceberg. Satanically-inspired philosophies of teaching and learning operational in our public schools today have the potential for decimating this generation and the next if we do not take appropriate action.

NEW AGE GOES TO SCHOOL

Just what philosophies are our children being taught in the classroom today? What values are they assimilating that are supposed to help them deal with life? One public school teacher attending a New Age seminar admitted that her teaching goal was "to help the children get in touch with their divinity. These things are crucial to our own evolution."[2] You can't completely comprehend the impact of this movement on the educational system until you recognize the many faces of the New Age in our public schools today.

Like many other institutions, including the U.S. Army, public education has tapped into the human potential movement of the 1960s for cost-effective training methods that reportedly enhance classroom performance. As a result, many of our public schools are implementing techniques that are rooted in Eastern mysticism, the New Age, and the occult, including guided imagery, meditation, biofeedback, neurolinguistic programming, and various other techniques designed to reduce stress and increase concentration.[3] Let's look at the impact this approach is making in our schools.

A New Vocabulary

Schools are gradually shifting the emphasis from cognitive skills (facts, information) to affective skills (feelings, attitudes). This new direction has been dubbed "therapy education" by some, and a new jargon has been designed to promote it. These terms include values clarification, behavior modification, moral reasoning, higher critical thinking, and holistic education. Techniques associated with these terms are being integrated into school curriculum.

These new terms simply mask old New Age ideas like yoga, meditation, and globalism so parents won't be alarmed. The apparent "innocence" of New Age educational terminology makes the ideas more acceptable. New Age activist Dick Sutphen states: "One of the biggest advantages we have as New Agers is, once the occult, metaphysical, and New Age terminology is removed, we have concepts and techniques that are very acceptable to the general public. So we can change the names to demonstrate the power. In doing so, we open the door to millions who normally would not be receptive."[4]

Values clarification is compatible with New Age thinking called "confluent education." This New Age theory posits the equality of individual values, because everyone has the wisdom of the universe within him. Remember: To the New Ager, truth is relative. So education is the process of helping each child discover *his* truth, since there is no absolute truth.

Jack Canfield, Director of Educational Services for Insight Training Seminars, is a strong proponent of holistic education. In his paper entitled, "The Inner Classroom: Teaching with Guided Imagery," he states:

> Guided imagery is a very powerful pyschological tool which can be used to achieve a wide variety of educational objectives: enhance self-esteem, expand awareness, facilitate psychological growth and integration, evoke a more positive attitude, and accelerate the learning of subject matter. . . . I hope you will attempt some of the suggestions I have presented you with here. If you do, you will embark upon a new and adventurous journey in your teaching. You can expect some profound changes to occur in our classroom, and in these days of stress and burnout, that's a nice thing to look forward to.[5]

As Canfield notes, New Age mind exercises like guided imagery and visualization are being used to achieve a wide variety of educational objectives: enhancing self-esteem, expanding awareness, facilitating psychological growth and integration, evoking a more positive attitude, and accelerating the learning of subject matter. Children are taught to visualize ideal situations as a step to realizing them. Guided imagery reflects the New Age tenet that reality is determined by what you believe.

Transcendental meditation practices are now being used under the guise of increasing self-esteem. In some schools kids are routinely sent to the school counselor's office to lie on the floor and breathe deeply. Then they empty their minds and meditate as they listen to a series of guided fantasy tapes. At times they are even led to participate in astral projection.[6]

Teachers are learning how to use fantasy role-playing games like Dungeons and Dragons to enhance student performance.. In one such game, "The Wizard," kids are taught to cast spells on each other. The purpose of the game is to progress from one "spell power" level to the next. Humans are at the lowest end of the spectrum, having very limited powers, and they are at the mercy of monsters. Higher levels include enchanters, sorcerers, magicians, and, of course, the Wizard.

The Holistic Truth

Shocking things are happening in the classroom in the name of holistic education. A Red Cross booklet on AIDS containing graphic descriptions of homosexual practices is being used on some campuses in science classes. Some teachers integrate units on lesbian history into their classes to help students become more accepting of "alternative lifestyles." Astrologers, palm readers, channelers (mediums), and even Tibetan monks are being invited into classrooms to "challenge" students, all in the name of critical thinking and understanding different worldviews.

Integrative education or transpersonal learning is being pushed by researchers as the optimum way to maximize classroom learning. Integrative education concludes that all things in the environment, including colors, sounds, textures, rhythms, shapes, objects, and other persons, are significant in the learning process. The "inner teacher" is one of the basic elements of the integrative approach. In theory, the best learning and performance come from the hidden teacher within each person. According to New Age educator Barbara Clark, "Integrative education has the capability to bring all of our knowledge, feelings, talents, and creativity into the classroom in the service of actualizing and transcending (a level of interconnectedness, the state of oneness with the universe that would include and use all of human functioning at its highest actualization).["7]

Many teachers are perpetuating New Age ideas without even realizing it. A great deal of effort has gone into luring teachers into the New Age perspective and encouraging them in their own "personal transformation." Training sessions encourage teachers, administrators, and counselors to get personally involved in the various techniques so they can experience firsthand the "wonders" they will be sharing with their students.

Many teachers today are being encouraged to transform their classrooms into laboratories to experiment on children rather than to emphasize basic life skills. What was once supposed to be a safe haven for learning has turned into an occultic mine field of indoctrination and conversion.

Hitting the Books

The days of Dick and Jane are long gone. The innocent storybooks children once used to learn how to read have been replaced by books containing stories that promote fear, violence, and occultic themes. This is especially horrifying when you realize that 75 percent of a student's classroom time and 90 percent of his homework time is spent with textbook materials.[8]

The National Institute of Education commissioned a systematic study of the content of public school textbooks. The conclusion was rather alarming: "Religion, traditional family values, and conservative political and economic positions have been reliably excluded from the children's textbooks."[9] Any educator can tell you that omitting these values from textbooks sends a very clear message to children: These values are unimportant because they were omitted. They are of lesser value than those which were included.

New Age educators are developing and testing curriculum at a feverish pace in hopes of gaining acceptance in school districts across the country. In order to be approved, these materials are cleverly being packaged as "scientific techniques" to help develop creativity, enhance learning capacity, and enable children to manage stress, solve problems, and improve self-esteem. How does the curriculum they produce measure up to these lofty goals? Here are some excerpts from the *Impressions* series published by Holt, Rinehart and Winston of Canada. *Impressions* is a comprehenseive language skills curriculum for first through sixth grades which is being marketed in all 50 states and across Canada.

> First graders are asked whether they would rather be crushed by a snake, swallowed by a fish, eaten by a crocodile, or sat on by a rhinoceros?
>
> Second graders see a drawing of a green creature whose long, sharp claws are gripping the head of a small child.
>
> *Under the Sea*, a third-grade reader, features an innocent-looking illustration entitled, "Shut the Windows, Bolt the Doors." The illustration shows floating objects: a refrigerator, a stove, a teddy bear, and a slice of pie. The manual instructs the teacher to have children write and chant spells to make things in the room float and then do the same thing to return the room to normal.
>
> In the fourth-grade reader, *Cross the Golden River*, kids read a poem entitled "Welcome," by sean o. huigin (who uses no capital letters in his name):

This is a poem for those who are brave
It starts at the mouth of a very old cave
A goblin will greet you as you walk in
His hair long and greasy and his green teeth
   agrin
His eyes red and tiny, his face grey and mean
He'll grab at your hand and let out a scream
He'll lead you down tunnels much darker than
   night
He'll take you past monsters that will try to
   bite
The toes off your footsies, the ears off your
   head
You soon will start wishing you'd stayed home
   in bed
Worms wet and slimy will crawl up your back
And as you go further it really gets black
You can't see a thing and all you can hear
Is a creaky old voice that says, "Come my dear
Let's see if you're chunky, let's feel if you're fat
I'm hungry today, NO STOP, DON'T GO
   BACK"
But if you are clever you'll get out of there
Or you'll end in some stomach no one knows
   where

Accompanying this reader is a student workbook that includes an exercise entitled "Three Spells." One spell it promotes is called "Zap." This spell supposedly shoots a blast of lightning from the child's hand. It is effective against virtually all living creatures who have no magical defenses.

Some people may think that an exercise in casting spells is an innocent "pretend" activity. But in the

Impressions teacher-resource books, the children are not told that the spells are "just pretend." Occult crime experts say that the spell-chanting found in *Impressions* is consistent with practices in the witchcraft religion of Wicca.

Sixth-grade students read about an abandoned infant who is found by three black-robed hags. One hag wonders what to do with him. The second croaks, "A sweet morsel, a tender lamb, I know what I should do."[10]

Much of this material is from the milder U.S.-Calgary version of *Impressions*. Other versions are the Canadian, the U.S.-Canadian, and the Calgary. Many of the editions sold in the United States in the last two years are the darker and scarier U.S.-Canadian version.

It is important to note that not everything in the *Impressions* series is offensive. Some textbooks include works by C.S. Lewis and Laura Ingalls Wilder.

The program *Developing Understanding of Self and Others (DUSO)*, published by American Guidance Service, St. Paul, Minnesota, contains 42 guided imagery lessons. Children are instructed to listen to a tape as they close their eyes and imagine they're traveling to strange planets and meeting friendly creatures. On one particular card (number 41) children are told they will be taking a trip to the land of "Aquatron." They are told to pretend they are using their bodies to show a stranger how they feel. Then they are to think about how they would act and picture themselves acting out their strong feelings. Finally they are to imagine that the other person understands how they feel.[11]

Another book approved for the classroom reading list is called *Sand Castles*, published by Harcourt, Brace, and

Jovanovich. One of the stories in the book is called "Race," dealing with cheating. The story concludes that cheating is okay if it is done to teach humility. Teachers are encouraged in the manual to use this story to promote decision-making.

Mission SOAR (Set Objectives, Achieve Results) was piloted in the Los Angeles school district to help reduce gang violence and build self-esteem in kids. Students were taught to communicate with the dead and receive guidance from their spiritual guides on how to plan their future lives. Mission SOAR very closely parallels the techniques found in *Beyond Hypnosis: A Program for Developing Your Psychic and Healing Powers,* by William W. Hewitt.[12]

Talented and gifted (TAG) children are of prime interest to New Agers for "conversion." The future of society rests with these kids, so they must receive specially focused indoctrination. Since TAG programs are generally open to experimentation they have become prime avenues for occult-oriented "transpersonal education." After all, what better place to work out the "bugs" before introducing the program into the mainstream of the educational system?[13]

Flights of Fantasy is a program used with gifted children. It is a form of guided imagery in which children imagine meeting strange creatures in space and merging with them before returning to earth.

DEALING WITH THE DANGERS
IN THE CLASSROOM

There is no question that materials like those cited above are damaging to the children who are subjected to them. Teachers say that materials like *Impressions* challenge a child's imagination and stretch his potential.

Others say it is effective in teaching language arts. But most of the content is too much for a young child's psyche. The frightening imagery overwhelms kids as they are asked to deal with issues they are ill-equipped to handle. And in the process they are being desensitized to the occult and the New Age. It is this subtle desensitization that we must protect our kids against.

With the mental and spiritual well-being of our children at stake, the real issue is not the good (but often misguided) intentions of teachers and administrators. Rather we must ask, "What does God's Word say about such practices?" Deuteronomy 18:10,11 clearly forbids many of the practices we have been discussing: "Let no one be found among you who sacrifices his son or daughter in the fire, who practices divination or sorcery, interprets omens, engages in witchcraft, or casts spells, or who is a medium or spiritist or who consults the dead" (NIV). Occult and New Age teaching methods are a danger to our kids because they oppose biblical guidelines. For example:

> *Confluent education* is dangerous because it leads kids to believe that they are divine and perfect. Since the sin problem is nonexistent, there is no need for Jesus Christ and what He accomplished on the cross. Being taught they are godlike, kids develop a false self-confidence.

> *Guided imagery* in the classroom is dangerous because it teaches children a way of dealing with problems that leaves God out of the picture. It can also open them up to the "angel of light" (2 Corinthians 11:14).

> *Visualization* is dangerous because it denies the lostness of man and the impact sin has on human imagination (Genesis 6:5).

Values clarification in the classroom is a menace because it denies the existence of moral absolutes from the Bible. Instead, each student is encouraged to come up with his own moral value system.

Eastern meditation in the classroom is perilous because kids are taught to empty their minds with the goal of attaining oneness with all things—"cosmic consciousness." Biblical meditation is much different because it always has the objective focus of filling the mind with the Word of God.

Globalism is threatening because it is based on a monistic worldview that promotes the unity of all mankind and all religious beliefs.

Yoga is dangerous because all of its forms involve occult assumptions, even hatha yoga which is often presented as a strictly physical discipline.

Homework for Parents

Perhaps you are a Christian parent, and your children are enrolled in a public school. How can you guard them and their fellow students against the subtle seduction of occultic and New Age materials and methods?

Paul's encouraging words in 1 Corinthians 16:13,14 are a good place to start: "Be on the alert, stand firm in the faith.... Let all that you do be done in love." It is important to keep these biblical principles in mind as you develop a strategy for handling the harmful influences impacting our educational system.

Here are some steps to consider for protecting your children against harmful practices in the classroom and replacing harmful materials and methods with those which are more positive.

1. Stay informed. Most parents don't have a clue about the materials and methods being used in their public schools. Contact your local school district office and ask for permission to review the curriculum being used. If your request is denied, file a complaint with the district. Do your homework. Be able to cite the specific dangers of offensive materials and methods. Earn the right to be heard by being thorough, well-prepared, and positive. In her book, *Child Abuse in the Classroom* (Crossway Books), Phyllis Schlafly provides a checklist to help parents evaluate school programs and materials (see pages 435-439).

2. Get involved. It's not enough for you to help with the cake sale and assist on an occasional school field trip. Get into your child's classroom as a volunteer aide. Observe what is taking place. Inform the teacher and the administration if you notice any questionable practices. Yes, it will cost you some time and effort to get involved at this level. But you must ask yourself, "Do I want to pay now or pay later?"

3. Gather support. Seek out curriculum experts, child psychologists, teachers, counselors, parents, pastors, and others who share your views. Develop a united task force and request a meeting with school or district administrators to discuss questionable curriculum and activities in the classroom. Be persistent.

4. Take action when necessary. If the administration rejects or ignores your requests, or if you have a one-sided, unproductive meeting, consider going to the school board.

Prepare your testimony, document your argument, and request everything in writing. If it appears that harmful curriculum will remain, request that alternative classes be established for children whose parents are opposed to the curriculum. Ask that a parental review panel be established to monitor quality in these alternative classes.

5. *Accept responsibility* for the parenting of your children. If kids are going to win in life, their most crucial need outside their personal relationship with Jesus Christ is strong parental support. You can only support your kids when you get personally involved in raising them. Their education isn't the school's job; it's your job. The school is merely helping you. And when the school hinders more than it helps, it's your job to correct the problem.

Similarly, your child's Christian education and growth isn't the church's job; it's your job. The church may provide support, but it is your responsibility to help your child develop a biblically-based worldview.

Let's do something before we lose an entire generation. Don't allow the complacency of our society to subtly restrain you. There is too much at stake. We can't afford to allow the themes of despair, occultism, mutilation, and witchcraft to become entrenched in the vulnerable minds of our children through our neglect. Jesus said, "It would be better for him to be thrown into the sea with a millstone tied around his neck than for him to cause one of these little ones to sin" (Luke 17:2 NIV).

Chapter 5

TOOLS OF THE
DEVIL'S TRADE

xxxxxxxxxxxxxxxxxxxxxxxxxxxxxxxxxxxxxxxxxxxxxxxxxxxxxx

I let an interest in Dungeons and Dragons become an obsession that later led me into Satanism," says 19-year-old Sean Sellers, found guilty of shooting his parents while they slept and now a death-row inmate in Oklahoma. "I performed rituals covered in blood, sometimes mixed with wine and urine, and began taking drugs. I thought I had at last found what I was looking for. I was wrong. Now as a result of all I did in Satanism, I am condemned to die."[1]

As a young boy Sean was exceedingly bright and spent a lot of time reading. First science fiction and stories of the supernatural held his attention. Later a baby-sitter introduced him to books about Satanism. Sean found himself strangely attracted to the occult. At the age of 12 he discovered the fantasy role-playing game Dungeons and Dragons.

But something else was going on in Sean's life during these formative years which sheds additional light on his slide from well-mannered child to morose adolescent.

Sean's parents were divorced when he was three. After his mother was remarried to a cross-country truck driver,

Sean was left in the care of a succession of family members while his parents traveled. Despite the sometimes long-distance relationship, Sean's mother and stepfather maintained rather strict control of his life. "Sean was never good enough.... They demanded more from him than any kid could give," said Jim Blackwell, Sean's grandfather. "He was a timid, beaten-down kid who had a need to be accepted. I can look back now and see where he was susceptible to anything."[2]

Though a dramatic extreme, Sean represents a generation of kids who are "susceptible to anything." Lack of hope for the future, the sad condition of our society, broken homes, disillusionment with God, the search for personal power, and the desire to be someone special are just some of the factors that make Satan's seduction to the dark side so appealing.

In this chapter we will explore a wide variety of the seductive tools Satan uses to draw our children away from God and their parents. Most kids who get involved in these schemes will never sink to Sellers' level. But once they are hooked on the supernatural, the potential to degenerate to total rebellion against parents, society, and God is always present.

FASHIONS FIT FOR THE FIRE

In the last 40 years teenagers have been famous for their unconventional clothes and hair, from the leather jackets and ducktails of the '50s to the bizarre punk styles of the '80s. But there are some subtle changes in the '90s. For many kids, clothing, make-up, and hairstyle are still outward signs of an inward struggle for acceptance and identity. But some of today's fashions seem to encourage a step into the darkness to meet these needs.

In one Southern California mall is a trendy shop geared for the younger generation. Over 95 percent of the items in the store sport satanic and occultic symbols (see Chapter 6 for an illustrated list of these symbols). They are embroidered, painted, or carved on belts, scarfs, jewelry, T-shirts, ties, pants, hats, and socks. The store is often packed with teens and preteens searching for the hottest "evil-looking" article to help them gain acceptance with the crowd at school. Even some of the major department stores are carrying these fashions.

There are two dangers in allowing your kids to wear fashions decorated with satanic and occultic symbols. First, the symbols represent values and a lifestyle that is contrary to the things of God. Second, in their desperate attempt to change their lives and overcome the pain of day-to-day living, kids will experiment with these symbols to see if there really is any power in them. As Sean Sellers discovered, kids who play around with these things often find more than they bargained for.

Some kids like to dress in black. Some even go so far as to dye their hair black, wear pale make-up accented in dark colors, and paint their fingernails black. Kids who are obsessed with black may be mirroring an unhealthy inner fascination with darkness. Those who are caught up in these fads may be subconsciously crying out, "Please help me!"

PLAYING WITH FIRE

Fantasy role-playing games have taken the nation by storm since their introduction in 1975 on college campuses. These games are an addictive escape from reality to the world of occultic mythology. Beginning as a fad among college students, fantasy role-playing games soon infected the more impressionable teen and preteen generation. By 1980, 46 percent of the fantasy games were purchased by 10- to 14-year-olds and 26 percent by 15- to 17-year-olds.[3]

What's wrong with fantasy role-playing games? Each game has its own distinctive characters, elements, and universe (theology or worldview). Players must use vivid imagination to assume the role of one of the game's characters, and most of the characters are bad: thieves, assassins, magic-users, etc. Through the course of a game, which can last for days, weeks, and even months, the player identifies more deeply with these sinister characters. Such intense exposure to evil affects a person's self-image and personality, and opens him to satanic influence. Since 1979 fantasy role-playing games have been linked with suicides, murders, and mysterious disappearances across the country.

The following games entice and encourage kids to experiment with the supernatural. They are closely linked with Satanism and the occult.

Parlor Games

Dungeons and Dragons. This is by far the most popular of the fantasy role-playing games. The objective is to maneuver characters through a maze of tunnels (dungeons) filled with ambushes, monsters, and magic in search of treasure. Three or more players can play, with the most important player being the Dungeon Master.

Characters are good and evil with the more evil and violent ones possessing the greater power and life expectancy. Players earn power based on the number of enemies and monsters they kill. A number of various aids enable characters to survive: magical weapons, spells, potions, daggers, battle and hand axes, magical trinkets, and swords. The game continues endlessly as characters are murdered or grow in power to demigod status.

How seductive is Dungeons and Dragons? Isaac Bonewits, a practicing witch, considered it such a good tool for instructing people in paganism that he wrote a special manual showing players how to move from the game into real sorcery. For convicted killer Sean Sellers, the game further fueled the darkness in his life and led him into the trap of Satan worship and the occult. Our research showed that 44 percent of the kids who play the game have compulsive thoughts to kill!

A young Colorado boy who was consumed by his Dungeons and Dragons character killed himself, leaving the following note:

> Upon reading these words you will know that I am dead. I have started the lonesome journey to the bowels of the earth. I travel that twisted road that winds its way down to the forsaken pit. It is time to meet my lofty maker! My destination will be the foot of the throne, where I will kneel and greet my father. . . . My father will spread his wings and welcome me to his and my real home.[4]

Blood Mary. We described one version of Bloody Mary in Chapter 2. Two other versions are also played in a dark bathroom and are just as inviting to demonic powers.

In one of them the player chants "bloody Mary, bloody Mary" until invisible claws scratch his face and draw blood. Another version, a pseudo out-of-body experience, is based on the movie *Poltergeist.* After chanting "bloody Mary" in the dark bathroom, the player allows his mind to enter the mirror and travel to a particular destination—a friend's house, a store, etc. Sometimes the friend even knows that the player is visiting him, if he is also doing the right chants.

It's amazing how many kids see this game as a cute trick, not realizing that this casual clash with the occult is a dangerous first step into the world of spiritism.

Nightmare on Elm Street. This game is based on the very successful movie series of the same name. In the movies, a character dreams he is killed by Freddy Krueger, and then actually dies. In the game, players must move their game pieces from the Nightmare side of the board to the Awake side before evil Freddy strikes. Matching cards carry rhymes from the movie like, "One, two, Freddy's coming for you. Three, four, better lock your door. Five, six, grab your crucifix." The best way to confront the menacing murderer is to flash a Freddy Krueger card, consigning him to burn alive.

Throughout the game Freddy Krueger is on a massive killing spree. He appears to have incredible strength. He is the embodiment of supernatural evil. Only by Freddy's tactics—violence, terror, and assault—can a player successfully elude death and win.

Ouija board. A sixth-grade teacher in Southern California made the headlines of his local paper when he refused to remove a Ouija board from his classroom. He saw nothing wrong with the game and felt his First Amendment rights were at stake. Concerned parents went to the school board calling for the game's removal.

The Ouija board (the name is simply a combination of the French and German words for yes) has been around in various forms since the sixth century B.C. The modern Parker Brothers game board has the numbers zero through nine, the alphabet, and the words *good, bye, yes,* and *no* printed on the surface. A teardrop-shaped pointer is placed on the board.

Two players face each other over the board with their fingers lightly resting on the pointer, allowing it to move freely. The players ask guidance questions relating to such things as career, marriage, investments, gambling, and health, and wait for the counter to spell out the answers. The game has also been used for contacting the dead and the living, contacting the spirit realm, developing psychic powers, and finding lost belongings.

How or why the game works is a mystery—even to the manufacturer. The instructions include the statement: "If you use it in a frivolous spirit, asking ridiculous questions, laughing over it, you naturally get undeveloped influences around you."[5] What are these "undeveloped influences"? Some of what happens on the board is from the subconscious mind of the operator. But some information reflects contact with demons, and the game has been linked to a variety of spiritual conflicts. Satanists have been known to crash Ouija board parties to help players learn how to "really use the game."

The Ouija board is clearly a form of divination which is repeatedly forbidden in Scripture.

I Ching or Book of Changes. This is an ancient Chinese volume of collective wisdom. It is consulted in conjunction with casting yarrow sticks or tossing coins. Patterns formed by the sticks or coins are said to reveal subconscious tendencies that the I Ching glyphs and hexagrams interpret spiritually and psychologically.

Tea Leaves. Tea leaves are read in the bottom of an empty cup. Occult lore holds that the cup corresponds to the dome of the sky, and the leaves are like stars in conjunctive configurations.

We have only scratched the surface in exploring parlor games with satanic and occultic orientation. There is a long list of occult-oriented games including Tunnels and Trolls, Chivalry and Sorcery, Runne Quest, Swordbearers, and Arduin Grimoire. In addition, we have no idea what other kinds of harmful games will be introduced in the future. Guard your child against an apparent recreational diversion which in reality may be a first step into the enemy's domain.

Computer/Video Games

Computer/video mania has captured our children even down to the preschool ages. Electronic game manufacturers are making millions of dollars from various computer/ video games that subtly lure kids into the kingdom of darkness. Here are a few examples of games dabbling in occult themes and what the manufacturers say about them.

> *Hero's Quest I.* "Create your own character from the ground up and venture forth into a world of magic. Become a mysterious magician, a fierce fighter, or a wily thief."

> *Hero's Quest III.* "Can you escape the bondage of the evil wizard Mannanan? . . . Learn to use magic . . . but don't get caught. . . . Find the amazing truth to your real identity."

> *Phantasie.* "When sorcery ruled and trolls still walked the earth."

Phantasie III: The Wrath of Nikademus. "This game boasts many new features including more potent spells, weapons, and character skills."

Wizard's Crown. "Guide your valiant band through detailed tactical battles with magic and mystery."

The Secret of the Silver Blade and *Dragon Strike.* Even Dungeons and Dragons has capitalized on the popularity of computer games with these two advanced versions.

Nintendo Games. Has a Nintendo Entertainment System found its way into your family room? Beware of games like Solstice, Final Fantasy, and Dream Master. They promote strong occultic and New Age themes.

In *Castlevania III: Dracula's Curse,* the player becomes Trevor Belmont, youthful hero and originator of the Belmont Warlord line. The instructions read: "Your task is to foil the schemes of the Middle Ages' ultimate evil, Count Dracula. You will not be alone in your quest to conquer the Count. Along the way, you'll encounter three companion spirits, each with special abilities, which you can enlist as your allies. Choose wisely the spirit you take along, for you can only have one accompany you at a time in your journey."

Altered Beast. Here is a description of this game from the Genesis Video Entertainment System: "Imagine being awakened from the grave to single-handedly defeat an entire horde of creatures from the Underworld.... But you will not descend into the dark world alone. With you goes the mythical power of the Altered Beast."

Games like these are more than just entertainment. They entice kids through the attraction of supernatural powers of magic and sorcery and become doorways for a child's first steps into Satanism, the occult, and New Age. We're not saying that all computer/video games are satanic. But you need to screen the games you allow in your home and weed out any that could tantalize your child to the dark side.

SCREAMS FROM THE SCREEN

"Slasher" movies have a broad following among kids today. These films flood the screen with inescapable terror, blood, gore, mutilation, and death. At the same time these films desensitize our kids to evil, making them easy targets for Satan who would seduce them to the same behavior.

Here's a sampling of some of the favorites among kids:

My Bloody Valentine depicts teenagers trapped in an abandoned mine where a crazed miner mutilates and kills them.

Prom Night shows a hooded killer haunting a high school prom. In one scene a severed head rolls across the dance floor.

Friday the 13th features a psychopathic killer named Jason who wears a hockey mask. Nineteen-year-old Mark Branch became so obsessed with Jason that he "wanted to see what it feels like to kill." Sharon Gregory, an acquaintance of Branch, was found stabbed to death in her bathtub. Police found video cassettes of *Friday the 13th* and a hockey mask in his home. Mark's dead body was later found hanging in the woods.[6]

Nightmare on Elm Street, the most successful horror film to date, features the incinerated child molester Freddy Krueger, who disembowels and decapitates his victims first in their dreams, then for real. Merchandise sales of Freddy Krueger masks, albums, books, games, and dolls have topped $15 million.[7]

A group of fourth, fifth, and sixth grade students at a Christian school were asked why they liked *Friday the 13th* and *Nightmare on Elm Street*. Here are some of their responses: "I like how Jason chops people's heads off"; "I like the way people look when they're dead"; "It's the violence and the weapons they use to kill people that I like most."

The Rocky Horror Picture Show is a musical based on transvestism, sadomasochism, and a host of other perversions. Theaters showing the movie have been frequented by Satanists to meet and recruit.

Films don't have to be of the blood-and-guts variety to be linked to spiritual darkness. A number of recent films are popularizing more subtle occultic themes:

Ghost is the story of how a young widow finds peace and love through a unique channel with her dead husband.

Flatliners shows a group of medical students experimenting with trips beyond the grave and back again.

Defending Your Life is the story of a dead man in limbo who must prove himself before going on to a new life.

Switch is about a man who is reincarnated as a woman.

One of the major fronts of Satan's seductive activity among our kids is movies and videos. One of the greatest dangers of these films is their ability to desensitize kids to evil, violence, and terror. We need to protect our kids from any foothold the enemy may seek to gain through this entertainment medium. Preview all films before you allow your children to see them. In this way you can help them "avoid every kind of evil" (1 Thessalonians 5:22 NIV).

TANTALIZED BY THE TUBE

Most people would agree that television has become the number one value-shaper in our country. The average person spends 23 to 26 hours per week in front of the tube. Studies indicate that the average young person will have watched 17,000 hours of television before graduating from high school. More time is spent in front of a television set than any other activity except for sleeping.

Television broadcasts a variety of programs with links to the occult. As a concerned parent you should be carefully screening everything your child watches from Saturday morning cartoons to movies of the week.

Innocent Saturday morning cartoons like Popeye and Mighty Mouse have given way to evil influences masked in cuddly characters that kids and parents find hard to resist. Sorcery, spells, incantations, power beams, ESP, crystal powers, telepathy, Eastern religions, and the "power of the rainbow" can be found in such programs as "The

Smurfs," "Gummi Bears," "He Man/She Ra," "Care Bears," "Teenage Mutant Ninja Turtles," and "My Little Pony."

The more popular cartoon shows have produced an unending stream of toys and merchandise: stuffed animals, clothing, dolls, games, bedding, and even snacks like macaroni and cheese and breakfast cereals. Bringing these items into the home and allowing your kids to act out the cartoon stories with them further entrenches ungodly influences in their minds and behavior.

Prime-time TV is also showing an increasing number of weekly shows and made-for-TV movies portraying occultic themes. For example:

> *Quantum Leap* pictures the exploits of a time-traveler inhabiting the bodies of different men and women in order to change their personal histories. The pseudohero is accompanied by a "guide."

> *Shades of L.A.* was an action drama featuring an L.A. detective who runs into some dead folks who have unfinished business on earth. These "shades" help the detective crack some tough cases, to the amazement of his colleagues.

> *Twin Peaks* was a popular show featuring an odd mixture of sex, murder, perversion, and intrigue. The show's hero received midnight visits from a king-sized spirit. Other characters were possessed by demented personalities and suicidal thoughts.

A child's naive fascination with darkness veiled as TV entertainment may encourage further steps into the occult. Remind your children of Philippians 4:8: "Whatever is true, whatever is noble, whatever is right, whatever is

pure, whatever is lovely, whatever is admirable—if anything is excellent or praiseworthy—think about such
things" (NIV).

CHEMICAL CATASTROPHES

Drug and alcohol abuse has reached epidemic propor-
tions in our society, especially among young people. The
average age of first drug use is 13, and it's 12 for first
alcohol use.[8] By the time young people graduate from high
school:

> Eighty-five percent have experimented with alcohol.
>
> Fifty-seven percent have tried an illicit drug.
>
> Thirty-three percent have smoked marijuana occa-
> sionally.
>
> Twenty-five percent have smoked marijuana regu-
> larly.
>
> Seventeen percent have tried cocaine or crack.[9]

Kids use and abuse drugs and alcohol for two main
reasons. First, drugs make them feel good. Everything
about their lives is changing so rapidly that they are often
filled with boredom, confusion, loneliness, alienation, and
unhappiness. Intoxicating substances are enchanting and
exhilarating, helping them dull the pain and pressure in
their lives. An 11-year-old cocaine addict said he had used
drugs "so I wouldn't have to feel anymore."

Second, drugs give kids a sense of security. The break-
down of the family and the uprooting kids experience
every couple of years as families move create insecurity.
Drugs and alcohol appear more dependable to them than

family or friends. Drugs are there when kids need them, and they work every time.

Mind-Control Substances

It's no coincidence that the rise in occultic activity among young people parallels the rise in substance abuse. There is a definite link between the two (although every young person using drugs isn't necessarily involved in the occult). Satan's goal is to capture a child's mind. Mind-altering substances leave kids vulnerable to his control. A 15-year-old girl summed it up this way: "Taking drugs is like getting into a strange car with a strange person and not knowing where you are going."

A direct correlation between drugs and Satanism has been repeatedly and dramatically demonstrated.

In 1989 five people were arrested in Matamoros, Mexico, in connection with the slaughter of 12 people. The victims were sacrificed and cannibalized by a satanic cult of drug smugglers.

Authorities in Los Angeles linked drugs, sexual perversion, and heavy metal music with the infamous Night Stalker case. Convicted killer Richard Ramirez cried out "Hail Satan" in a crowded courtroom and displayed a pentagram drawn on his hand.

Jim Hardy, of Carl Junction, Missouri, began experimenting with drugs as a sixth grader and was hooked by age 13. He and two friends forged a blood-brother relationship around drugs, heavy metal music, gory movies, witchcraft, and Satanism. At age 17 they committed a human sacrifice. Jim later explained, "I would kind of just pray to God and Satan at the same

time to see who was more powerful, and little by little
I fell out of God and started falling into Satan.... You
can't just dabble. It sucks you in real quick."[10]

I received a phone call from a mother who was filled with
anxiety and pain. "Steve, you've got to help me," she pleaded.
"I just found a loaded gun, a bag of narcotics, and an altar
to Satan in my teenage son's bedroom. I don't know what to
do."
"How long have these things been in his room?" I asked.
"I don't know," she said. "It's been months since I've
been in his room or had a real conversation with him."
Unfortunately, there are many parents like this mother.
They spend so little time with their children that they
are unaware of the symptoms of substance use and abuse.
The more involved and communicative you are with your
child, the more you will protect him against the seduction
of substances and the steps into darkness they encourage.

DANCING IN THE DARK

Music is second only to television in influencing and
shaping the values of our children. The average teenager
listens to 10,500 hours of rock music between the seventh
and twelfth grades. And since 1981 an entire generation
has been growing up on MTV (music television) and music
videos. According to Brandon Tartikoff, president of NBC
Entertainment, "MTV is an institution. There is a whole
generation out there molded and influenced by it."[11]
Music not only reflects the youth culture, it directs it as
well. Dr. James Dobson says, "It is difficult to overestimate
the negative impact music is having. Rock stars are the
heroes, the idols that young people want to emulate."[12]

Rock music and those who perform it often focus on themes like sex, Satanism, drugs, and violence. Popular groups today sing about women being raped, hatred for police, and racial violence. During their concerts, some heavy metal groups mimic masturbation or use satanic images on stage. Even if your kids don't agree with the lyrics and only listen "for the beat," overexposure to these personalities and themes may corrupt their values and open them to demonic powers.

Lyrics from the Pit

The harvest of occult themes in contemporary music can be traced to seeds planted by some of the earliest rock stars. The Rolling Stones recorded songs like "Sympathy for the Devil," "Their Satanic Majesties' Request," and "Goat's Head Soup" (a severed goat's head is used in satanic worship). Former Black Sabbath lead singer Ozzy Osbourne sang openly of demons in "The Devil's Daughter." Osbourne argues, "I'm not a maniac devil-worshiper. I'm just playing the role and having fun with it."

Richard Ramirez, the Night Stalker, is said to have been obsessed with the satanic themes in the album, *Highway to Hell*, by heavy metal band AC/DC. His favorite song was "Night Prowler," about slipping into the room of unsuspecting women. Pentagrams were painted on the walls in the rooms of some of his victims.

The lyrics of current heavy metal and black metal bands are even more perverse and satanic, dealing with such topics as the death of God, sitting at Satan's left hand, sex with corpses, calling Jesus Christ the deceiver, human sacrifice, and glorifying the names of Satan. And the lyrics are getting through. An Arkansas teenager attempted to kill his parents with a club and a butcher knife under the inspiration of a song by the heavy metal band Slayer. The boy said he consulted a Ouija board and heard voices telling him to murder his parents. Police found his cassette player cued to a Slayer song titled "Altar of Sacrifice."

Few of the metal bands admit to being Satan-worshipers, contending that their satanic symbols and lyrics are nothing more than a sales gimmick. But Dea Lucas, a high priestess in the Church of Satan in Van Nuys, California, claims that heavy metal is a prime recruiting tool: "Heavy metal groups are influencing the kids to come to Satan.... The groups are into Satanism even though they may deny it. Just by listening to the lyrics, being a satanist myself, I can read between the lines."[13]

Dr. Paul King, a child psychiatrist in Memphis, Tennessee, believes that music influences kids: "The kids I've seen who are violent and into drugs by and large are into heavy metal..... The music doesn't make them do it, but the lyrics become their philosophy."[14]

The musicians themselves are as influential as the lyrics. In 1991, pop music icon Madonna, who's been banned on MTV, blasted by the Vatican, and almost arrested for simulating masturbation on stage, released a provocative film titled *Truth or Dare*. The film details her controversial behavior during her "Blonde Ambition" tour. Near the end of the film she laments, "I'm a tormented person. I have a lot of demons inside of me. My pain is as big as my joy."[15] Unfortunately, Madonna is idolized by thousands of young girls who live as "Madonna-wanna-be's."

Keeping Your Kids in Tune

How can you help your kids recognize the subtle seduction to evil in contemporary music and encourage them to wise choices about what they listen to? Here are some practical suggestions:

1. Avoid the "do as I say, not as I do" syndrome. Before you can help your child evaluate his music, you'd better evaluate your own (Matthew 7:4,5). The lyrics of some soft rock, easy listening, and country-western tunes are as suggestive and immoral as those performed by heavy metal groups. One of the best ways to teach your child to avoid harmful lyrics is by modeling the same behavior.

2. Be willing to find middle ground. Your personal taste in music should not be the determining factor for what you allow your children to listen to. Nor should your child's taste determine what you listen to. Try to find some middle ground with your child when it comes to the kinds of music you will allow in your home. The key is to teach your child to be moderate and discerning, just as you are.

3. Stay informed and involved. When was the last time you looked through your child's music collection or sat down with him to listen to and discuss the lyrics of his favorite songs? You won't be able to understand the impact of the music in his life unless you are aware of it and what he thinks about it.

First Thessalonians 5:21 encourages us to "examine everything carefully." The following questions will help you help your child apply this principle to the music in his life. But remember: You must also respond to these questions as they relate to your music if you want your child to do so with his music.

How much time each week do you spend in the following: listening to music? watching TV (including MTV)?

attending school? visiting with friends? reading or studying your Bible? praying? Based on your answers, who or what is having the greatest influence on your thought life? What are some more positive, creative ways you could spend your time?

How does the music you listen to make you feel? What does it make you think about? Are these the kinds of feelings and thoughts you should be entertaining? Why or why not?

What are your favorite styles of music? What themes or subjects are communicated by your favorite artists or bands in each category?

Who are your favorite singers and musicians? Why do you like their music? What do their personal lives demonstrate about their values? Do you agree with their values? Why or why not?

Have you ever done something because you got the idea from a popular song (dress, hairstyle, language, etc.)? Are you aware that music affects your thoughts and feelings, which in turn determine your behavior?

Read Philippians 4:8, then read the lyrics of some of your favorite songs. Which songs fit the guidelines of this biblical principle? Which songs don't fit these guidelines?

These questions, discussed with your children in a loving, reciprocal way, will help them develop a solid, practical strategy for evaluating the music they listen to. Take time to listen to their emotional struggles and notice how the music they listen to influences their behavior. Be as encouraging about their good choices of music as you are corrective of the bad choices. Some day they will thank you for the harmony you helped bring to their lives.

Chapter 6

SYMPTOMS AND SIGNS
OF SEDUCTION

xxxxxxxxxxxxxxxxxxxxxxxxxxxxxxxxxxxxxxxxxxxxxxxxxxxxxxxxxxxxxxxxxx

After reading the last chapter you may be saying to yourself, "My child is a good kid. He's not into stuff like Satanism, the occult, or drugs." Hopefully you're right. But if he was dabbling in darkness and drugs, would you know it? Remember: Satan is a deceiver. If he is seducing your child in these areas, he doesn't want him or you to know about it.

We share with you now some of the symptoms and warning signs of possible involvement in Satanism, the occult, and drugs. (A glossary of satanic/occultic terms and nine statements of satanic doctrine are found in the Appendix.) If your child exhibits any of the following behaviors or possessions, don't jump to conclusions too quickly or react too slowly to the potential danger. Be prayerful, cautious, concerned, and ready to act. Part Three will give you some specific responses for helping a child who has been seduced into darkness.

SYMPTOMS OF POSSIBLE INVOLVEMENT
IN SATANISM AND THE OCCULT

A child's involvement in satanic/occult activities usually

begins with a morbid curiosity that prompts him to dabble in the supernatural. When curious involvement continues unchecked it eventually leads to serious involvement and ultimately rebellion. Watch for the following symptoms and deal with them appropriately.

Symptoms of Curious Involvement

Withdrawal from routine activities. Be aware of unusual seclusion and secrecy by your child, and a lack of accountability for his whereabouts.

Obsession with death and suicide. Pay attention to the music your child listens to and the videos he watches, especially those that glorify violence, destruction, and death. Also make note of scribbles and doodles on notebooks and book covers that portray these themes.

Extremely low self-image. Watch for frequent, unexplainable outbursts of anger or dramatic mood swings. Also note evidence of disillusionment in your child which is evidenced in sloppy appearance and a preference for being alone.

Inordinate disinterest in school and/or church. A severe drop in grades is an indication that something is wrong, as is excessive boredom and an apparent abandonment of school activities. A sudden change in a child's belief system is another warning sign. He may display this through consistent questioning of certain Scripture passages or a hostile attitude toward Christianity.

Obsession with black. Your child may manifest this obsession by dying his hair black, wearing dark make-up to an extreme, or dressing in black. Be careful not to overreact, however, if black is also an "in" color in your child's culture.

Radical change in friends. Be aware of who your child's friends are and what they are involved in. Watch for signs of secretive behavior, a disinterest in being with family members or old friends, and a rejection of parental values.

Fixation with satanic/occultic symbols. These symbols can be found on a variety of items including clothing and jewelry, album covers, toys, games, etc. Many of these symbols are pictured and explained later in this chapter.

Possession of "how to" satanic literature. These include the satanic bible, books like *Magick*, by Allister Crowley, manuals on how to cast spells, etc.

Involvement with satanic/occultic items. These include games, toys, movies, music (especially black metal and heavy metal), etc.

Drug and/or alcohol use. Many kids today are ready to try anything to get high. It may seem innocent, like spraying large doses of breath freshener to get a buzz from the alcohol content. Or it may be bizarre and dangerous, like diluting cocaine in eye drops and applying it to the eyes. Several symptoms of involvement with drugs are listed later in this chapter.

Excessive fear or anxiety. Most young people express concern from time to time over the world situation (wars, natural disasters, etc.). But you have cause for concern if your child exhibits unusual preoccupation and paranoia about current events.

Symptoms of Serious Involvement

Fascination with or possession of knives. Knives of various sizes and shapes are used in satanic rituals, black masses, and sacrifices. It is usually obvious if your child's interest is deeper than an innocent collection. Be especially aware of daggers.

Candle wax drippings. Candles are an important part of satanic rituals. Be alert to drippings on clothing, carpet, etc. Generally the wax will be black, red, or white.

Religious artifacts and bells. Watch for articles that are used in satanic rituals, such as chalices, goblets, bells, gongs, and even communion wafers. Bells and gongs are used to purify the air and dismiss the demons at the conclusion of the ceremony.

Cuts, scratches, burns, and tattoos. Look for scars or tattoos in the shape of satanic symbols on hidden parts of the body. In the extreme, watch for missing fingers and toes. Any unusual health problems should be thoroughly investigated.

Books and journals. Watch for books, drawings, poetry, diaries, and other forms of written communication that focus on death, the occult, Satan-worship, black magic, reincarnation, or witchcraft. Anything written in blood, backward script, secret code, or homemade alphabet could be connected to the occult.

Satanic altars. They can be simple or elaborate, located in a bedroom, closet, basement, or attic. Often they are illuminated by black, red, or white candles and decorated with ritual knives and possibly even animal bones.

SATANIC/OCCULTIC SYMBOLS

Watch for these symbols printed, drawn, sewn, or carved on your child's possessions. He may not realize that they are connected with Satanism and the occult. Help him understand that a preoccupation with these symbols and what they represent is an invitation to spiritual problems.

 Anarchy. Represents the abolition of all law and the denial of authority. Initially, those into punk music used this symbol. Now it is widely used by the followers of heavy metal music and self-styled satanists.

 Ankh. An ancient Egyptian symbol of life often associated with fertility. The top portion represents the female, and the lower portion symbolizes the male.

 Anti-justice. The Roman symbol for justice was an upright double-bladed ax. The representation of anti-justice inverts the double-bladed ax.

 Black mass indicators. These signs can be used as a source of direction as well as a sign of involvement in black masses.

 Blood ritual. Represents human and animal sacrifices.

 Cross of confusion. An ancient Roman symbol questioning the existence or validity of Christianity.

 Cross of Nero. Represented peace in the '60s. Among today's heavy metal and occult groups it signifies the defeat of Christianity (an inverted cross with the cross anchor broken downward).

Diana and Lucifer. The moon goddess Diana and the morning star Lucifer are found in nearly all types of witchcraft and satanism. When the moon faces the opposite direction, it is primarily a satanic symbol.

 Hexagram. Also referred to as the seal of Solomon, the hexagram is said to be one of the most powerful symbols in the occult.

 Horned Hand. A sign of recognition among those in the occult. It is also used by those attending heavy metal concerts to affirm allegiance to the music's message of negativism.

 Mark of the beast. Four different representations of the mark of the beast or Satan. Note that the letter *F* is the sixth letter in the alphabet.

 Pentagram. A five-pointed star, with or without the circle, is an important symbol in most forms of magic. Generally, the top point represents the spirit and the other points represent wind, fire, earth, and water.

 *Sample altar.* The altar may be any flat object where the implements of the ritual are placed. Usually the altar will be placed within a nine-foot circle. It could be as large as 48 inches long, 22 inches wide, and two inches high. The pentagram in the center is etched into the slab. Human or animal blood is then poured into the etching. Other symbols may be carved according to individual group traditions. Implements on the altar may include: chalice, candles, parchment, cauldron, and the *Book of Shadows.* A smaller version of the altar can be found in the bedrooms, closets, etc. of young, self-styled satanists or dabblers.

Swastika (broken cross). A symbol of ancient origin, it originally represented the four winds, the four seasons, and the four points of the compass. At that time its arms were at 90-degree angles turned the opposite direction as depicted here. The swastika shown here represents the elements or forces turning against nature and out of harmony. Neo-Nazis and occult groups use it in this manner.

 Talisman or amulet. An object with the name or image of a god drawn or inscribed in it.

 Triangle. May vary in size, but it is generally inscribed or drawn on the ground as the place where a demon would appear in a conjuration ritual.

 Upside-down pentagram. Sometimes called a baphomet, it is strictly satanic and represents a goat's head.

Symptoms of Possible Drug or Alcohol Use

Drug and alcohol use causes certain behavioral changes in kids. Below are some signs which may indicate a possible problem with drugs or alcohol.

Time distortion. Kids have difficulty waking up and being on time for appointments.

Diminished attention to hygiene and appearance. They avoid grooming themselves, or they wear dirty and/or unattractive clothes. They maintain a generally poor appearance.

Lack of motivation and concentration. They display little initiative or drive for chores, schoolwork, and even recreation. They are mistake-prone or sloppy. Their grades drop drastically.

Sudden mood swings. They swing from depression to happiness and back again in minutes. They are subject to outbursts of anger and experience increased anxiety.

Withdrawal. They are quiet and pull away from family members. Old friends drift away. They limit their social activities.

Change in religious values. They drop out of church activities and become inconsistent in personal devotions.

Telltale clothes. They display a preference for T-shirts, caps, etc. that glorify drinking or drugs.

Possession of suspicious substances. You discover subtances in their rooms you can't identify: powders, pills, leafy materials, small crystalline rocks, etc.

Unusual hostility or distrust. They treat you like an enemy and begin locking their rooms or hiding things from you.

Valuables begin to disappear. You notice cash missing from your wallet, purse, or cookie jar. Family items which can be sold for drug or alcohol money also disappear. Their own personal effects suddenly increase or decrease greatly.

STAY ALERT

In light of the arsenal of deceptive, seductive, and harmful weapons at Satan's disposal, there are several important factors you should keep in mind.

Evil is "in" today with kids. Everywhere they go, kids are confronted with how "cool" it is to be bad. A professional skateboarder was asked why his personalized line of skateboards contained graphics of strange human figures dancing in front of a fire with a wizard looming overhead. He said, "To sell boards, you have to offer something that looks evil. That's what kids like." We must constantly remember that we are in a spiritual battle and that our kids are a primary target for the enemy.

Christian kids are especially vulnerable to satanic influence. I was discussing with a public school counselor the increasing problem of students dabbling in occult practices on her campus. I asked her to give me a profile of the typical young person who is involved in the occult. "Oh, that's easy, Steve," she responded. "They're all church kids. They've had just enough of a taste of the supernatural to make them curious."

One concerned mother asked me, "What gives Satan the right to try to come into a Christian home?" He doesn't have that right. But he takes every opportunity you and your children offer him through your ignorance of his schemes.

One symptom doesn't mean your child is becoming a Satan-worshiper. If you suspect that your child is involved in occultic activity at some level, look into the situation with an open mind. It may be the beginning of a real problem, or it may just be your child's search for identity and acceptance.

Avoid looking for a quick fix. After speaking to a group of Christian parents about helping their kids resist Satan's seductive activity, one mother said, "Steve, what you shared was good, but it takes so much time. Isn't there an easier way?" That's the cry of our society. We want a Band-Aid approach to critical issues and problems. In order to win the spiritual battle for your child's mind, you need to invest your time and effort. And the best return for your investment will be realized if you start giving before the symptoms occur.

Look for root causes and real needs. If your child is purposely dabbling in Satanism and the occult it's probably because something is missing from his life. Some unmet need has prompted his spiritual conflict, and he's searching for answers in the wrong places. Begin looking for ways you can help meet his need in a positive way. Parts Two and Three of this book will help you do so.

PART 2

xxxxxxxxxxxxxxxxxxxxxxxxxxxxxxxxxxxxxxxxxxxxxxxxxxxxxxxxxxxxxxxxxxxxxxxxxxxxxxxxxxxx

The Effective Parent

xxxxxxxxxxxxxxxxxxxxxxxxxxxxxxxxxxxxxxxxxxxxxxxxxxxxxxxxxxxxxxxxxxxxxxxxxxxxxxxxxxxx

Chapter 7

Do You Really Know Who You Are?

Ten-year-old Matthew is a great kid. He's fun to be around, and he usually has a positive attitude. Matthew also has excellent athletic abilities. He loves to play baseball and has been in Little League since he was six years old.

But last year, whenever Matthew struck out he really got down on himself. By the end of the season he began to act out his negative feelings by disengaging from the game mentally. No amount of encouragement would cheer him up. At the same time he became fearful of being left home alone and especially of sleeping alone in his room. He slipped into a depression that frightened his parents. He seemed distant and detached from reality. Just putting Matthew to bed was an agonizing experience. His parents had to spend an inordinate amount of time assuring him that the house was secure and that he was safe.

Three weeks into Matthew's depression his parents attended one of my classes on resolving spiritual conflicts at Talbot School of Theology. By the end of the class they knew that Matthew was under demonic attack. The father explained in a letter:

Neil,

I took Matthew out for a walk Friday evening after the class was over and asked him if he felt hopeless. He said yes. He also said he was scared but didn't know why. I held him and we prayed for several minutes. I shared with him about his identity in Christ and his secure relationship with his Heavenly Father. I told him about his authority in Christ to stand against the enemy. Have you ever wondered if a 10-year-old boy can relate to this material? He was all ears!

I led him through a modified version of the Steps to Freedom in Christ I learned in the class. I shared with him how he could stand against Satan at home in his room. From that moment Matthew was a different boy. His whole countenance changed. The depression lifted immediately. His fear at night gradually disappeared as he began standing against Satan in Jesus' name. I believe Matthew now knows what it means to be a child of God. No longer is his identity wrapped up in his performance. He really seems to be free, and it is incredible to watch him grow in his relationship with the Lord.

It's all too easy for children like Matthew to find their identity wrapped up in external values like performance and appearance. Why? Largely because those are the values their parents and teachers glorify and reinforce. Kids today are applauded if they're cute, if they say funny things, or if they hit home runs. Thanks to the adults in their lives, it doesn't take long for kids to internalize and begin to live by three pervasive principles:

If I am physically attractive and others admire me, I will be special.

If I perform well and accomplish great things, I will be accepted.

If I obtain social status and others recognize me, I will be significant.

But what about the child who isn't very cute or entertaining? What about the child who never wins a starring role in the school play or who strikes out most of the time? Tragically, kids like these are often criticized or ignored by the adults in their lives. They begin to question their identity and doubt their worth. And then, as Matthew and his parents discovered, Satan can take advantage of the false values our society promotes. As we discussed in the opening paragraphs of Chapter 1, if Satan can confuse your child regarding his identity in Christ, he has a foothold in your child and in your home.

PARENTS IN IDENTITY CRISIS

One of the main reasons children struggle with identity and self-acceptance is because their parents are still struggling with the same issues. Both of Matthew's parents came from dysfunctional homes where their value as children was judged on the basis of appearance, performance, and status among their peers. Children who grow up with these false principles for identity and acceptance don't automatically grow out of them when they reach adulthood. As adults they continue to base their identity on these external guidelines and tend to perpetuate them in their children. If you are going to help your child realize his identity and acceptance in Christ and resist the devil, you must lead the way by doing so in your own life.

Identifying with the Natural World

Since you came into this world without Christ in your life, you learned to live independent from God. Your identity and purpose for living were found in the natural world. But no matter how hard you try to establish your identity and sense of purpose through your appearance, performance, or social status, you will always crumble in the face of rejection, criticism, introspection, guilt, worry, and doubt. Why? Because you were created to find fulfillment in Christ, not in temporal possessions or worldly achievement. Your self-image shouldn't hinge on being elected CEO of the company, chairman of the deacon board, or president of the PTA.

If you seek your identity or sense of worth in the temporal values of this world instead of in Christ, your family can become a threat to your pursuits in the following three ways.

Appearance. What image is more appealing to a woman: a youthful, athletic figure or the sometimes sagging frame of a responsible mother? Say goodbye to the bikini with those stretch marks! I've never heard of a beauty contest for pregnant mothers. Mothers who are hooked on appearances may end up resenting their children for robbing them of their girlish figure.

Some couples are agitated that their toy-strewn, baby-proofed house is never as attractive as the house of their DINK (*D*ouble *I*ncome, *N*o *K*ids) neighbors. They hate the fact that the backyard is the neighborhood's playground instead of a lovely botanical garden. Those who insist that the house must always be a showcase run the risk of sending their children an early message: The house is more important than you are. A sterilized house is rarely a warm home.

Then there are the nice clothes the young swinger can afford but you can't. And the sports car you drove when you were single is now a minivan with fingerprints all over the windows. If you are basing your self-worth on appearance, your family may be your worst enemy.

Performance. If you as a husband/father get your identity from your work, your primary goal may be to climb the corporate ladder. That means working some evenings and weekends to get ahead. "I'd like to be at your Little League game, Son," you say, "but I can't. I'll make it up to you later." Only later may be too late in some cases.

The pressure to perform is intense in today's business world. The boss says, "If you can't do the job, I'll get someone who can." The single men and women at the office are willing to work the extra hours. How can a responsible father or mother compete when he or she has family obligations at home? It is very easy to rationalize, "I'm the bread-winner around here. My family needs me to get ahead so we can have all the good things in life—luxury cars, suburban home, great vacations, ski boat, motor home, etc." Is the family going to help or hinder the performance-oriented man or woman?

What about performing well as a husband/father or wife/mother? Granted, few outside your home will see that performance. But God will and your children will! And in 20 years the world will see the results of your performance in the lives of your godly, well-adjusted children.

Status. Getting married and having children used to offer a woman favorable social status. Now a wife/mother is "just" a housewife. A status-seeking woman will see her family as a bother or hindrance. "I have to find myself in a challenging job where I can be creative and free from the responsibilities of child-raising," she argues. This is the driving force behind pro-choice advocates. They want the freedom to have sex without the responsibility of having children. "An unwanted child will utterly ruin my social life!"

But what's wrong with being a responsible, caring mother? What can be more challenging and satisfying than raising godly children today? Perhaps it's too challenging for some; that's why they are opting out. If your identity is attached to your position in society, your children may suffer as a result.

Identifying with Your Child's Achievements

"Then the mother of the sons of Zebedee came to Him [Jesus] with her sons, bowing down, and making a request of Him. . . . 'Command that in Your kingdom these two sons of mine may sit, one on Your right and one on Your left'" (Matthew 20:20,21).

Mrs. Zebedee was not the first or last mother to seek status, significance, and identity through a child's achievements. Parents who do such things are at best using their child and at worst abusing him. The child will cooperate initially because he longs for his parents' approval. But it won't be long before he sees through the sham: "Do you want me to be good for my sake or your sake? Do you care about me or only about your reputation?"

A pastor friend of mine came face-to-face with a parent's worst fear: His teenage daughter had become pregnant

before marriage. Perry was struggling with prickly questions: Should he resign his pastorate? Should he encourage an abortion to cover his embarrassment and save face?
Should he put her on the pill to avoid future problems?

I reminded him, "The primary goal for your life—to be
the father and husband that God's wants you to be—has
not been blocked by this unfortunate event. Your first
obligation is to your wife, your daughter, and her unborn
child. If there was ever a time that your wife needs a godly,
committed husband and your daughter needs a loving,
supportive father, it's now."

"But, Neil, what about being the pastor that God wants
me to be?" Perry argued. "Doesn't this disqualify me from
being a pastor?"

I directed him to one of the requirements for an elder in
1 Timothy 3:4,5: "He must be one who manages his own
household well, keeping his children under control with all
dignity (but if a man does not know how to manage his own
household, how will he take care of the church of God?)."

I said, "Even the best managers in the world have problems; they just know how to manage them. You didn't
instruct your daughter to sleep with her boyfriend. That
was a sinful decision she made. How are you going to
manage your home now for the good of your family? Instructing your daughter to get an abortion so you can save
face is mismanagement. Kicking her out of the house is
mismanagement. Trying to cover up the ugly incident is
mismanagement. Providing her with birth control pills to
avoid public disgrace is mismanagement. But standing by
your daughter, comforting your wife, walking in the light,
and speaking the truth in love is managing your household well."

Another pastor overheard my conversation with Perry.
"Man, that sobered me!" he said. "I'm going home and play

some games with my children tonight. If that happened to me in my church, I'd be out of the ministry."

I asked, "Is that why you want to play with your children, so they will be good and you can stay in ministry? Don't you want to play with your children because they are your children and you love them and desire to be with them?"

If you link your identity with your child's behavior, the devil will have a field day with your kids! Satan is the father of lies (John 8:44). His blueprint for the destruction of the home and the church is to get Christians to walk in the darkness (John 3:19,20). He wants you to play the "how do I look?" game instead of serving and managing your family. He schemes to make your acceptance among your Christian peers a matter of how well you appear and perform as a parent, and how few problems you have with your children. He'll try to convince you that being real carries the penalty of being rejected by others.

YOUR REAL IDENTITY IN CHRIST

Your verification as a believer does not come from outward appearance, performance, or social status. Your identity comes from being a child of God. Your sense of worth comes not from self, but from being in the image of God. Show me a person who knows who he is as a child of God, and I will show you a secure person who doesn't struggle with an identity crisis. When you realize that Christ is in you and your are in Christ, you won't worry any longer about self-image. Read through the following scriptural statements and see how your significance, acceptance, and security are all based on who you are in Christ.

In Christ I Am Significant

I am the salt of the earth (Matthew 5:13).

I am the light of the world (Matthew 5:14).

I am God's child (John 1:12; Romans 8:14-16; 1 John 3:3).

I am a branch of the true vine, a channel of His life (John 15:1,5).

I have been appointed to bear fruit (John 15:16).

I am Christ's personal witness (Acts 1:8).

I am God's temple (1 Corinthians 3:16).

I am a member of Christ's body (1 Corinthians 12:27).

I am a minister of reconciliation for God (2 Corinthians 5:17,18).

I am God's co-worker (1 Corinthians 3:9; 2 Corinthians 6:1).

I am a saint (Ephesians 1:1).

I have been raised up and seated with Christ (Ephesians 2:6).

I am God's workmanship (Ephesians 2:10).

I am a citizen of heaven (Ephesians 2:6; Philippians 3:20).

In Christ I Am Accepted

I am Christ's friend (John 15:15).

I have been justified (Romans 5:1).

I am joined to the Lord and am one spirit with Him (1 Corinthians 6:17).

I have been bought with a price; I belong to God (1 Corinthians 6:20).

I have been made righteous (2 Corinthians 5:21).

I have been adopted as God's child (Ephesians 1:5).

I have direct access to God through the Holy Spirit (Ephesians 2:18).

I am of God's household (Ephesians 2:19).

I am a fellow citizen with the rest of the saints (Ephesians 2:19).

I may approach God with boldness and confidence (Ephesians 3:12).

I have been redeemed and forgiven of all my sins (Colossians 1:14).

I am complete in Christ (Colossians 2:10).

In Christ I Am Secure

I am assured that all things work together for good (Romans 8:28).

I cannot be separated from the love of God (Romans 8:35).

I am free forever from condemnation (Romans 8:1).

I am free from any condemning charges against me (Romans 8:33).

I have been established, anointed, and sealed by God (2 Corinthians 1:21,22).

I have been given the Holy Spirit as a pledge guaranteeing my inheritance to come (Ephesians 1:13,14).

I have been delivered from the domain of darkness and transferred to the kingdom of Christ (Colossians 1:13).

I am hidden with Christ in God (Colossians 3:3).

I am confident that the good work that God began in me will be perfected (Philippians 1:6).

I can do all things through Him who strengthens me (Philippians 4:13).

I have not been given a spirit of fear, but of power, love, and a sound mind (2 Timothy 1:7).

I can find grace and mercy in time of need (Hebrews 4:16).

I am born of God, and the evil one cannot touch me (1 John 5:18).

All in a Family

Once you have a grasp on your identity in Christ, you need to express your godly character in your relationships. Your family is the primary laboratory for your personal development. This is precisely the order of Scripture: Establish your identity in Christ, then focus on living out who you are at home. Notice the order in Colossians 3:10-25:

> God's great goal for His children is that we conform to His image: "Put on the new self who is being renewed to a true knowledge according to the image of the One who created him" (verse 10).

> Our identity is no longer in racial, religious, cultural, or social ties: "A renewal in which there is no distinction between Greek and Jew, circumcised and uncircumcised, barbarian, Scythian, slave and freeman, but Christ is all, and in all" (verse 11).

Character is the focus of development once identity is established: "And so, as those who have been chosen of God, holy and beloved, put on a heart of compassion, kindness, humility, gentleness, and patience" (verse 12).

Character is developed in the context of relational living: "Bearing with one another, and forgiving each other, whoever has a complaint against any one, just as the Lord forgave you, so also should you" (verse 13).

Love is the highest level of character development: "And beyond all these things put on love, which is the perfect bond of unity" (verse 14).

The means by which all this is accomplished is Christ in you: "Let the peace of Christ rule in your hearts. . . . Let the word of Christ richly dwell within you with all wisdom" (verses 15-17).

The primary setting for character development is the home: "Wives, be subject to your husbands. . . . Husbands, love your wives. . . . Children, be obedient to your parents. . . . Fathers, do not exasperate your children" (verses 18-21).

You will see the same order in Ephesians and 1 Peter. As a parent, you are not just shaping your child's behavior, you are developing his character. Training a child doesn't mean smashing his will into oblivion; it means discipling him to be Christ-like as you are. Discipling is an 18-year process of letting go. Children need models, not critics (Luke 6:40). You can't model perfection, but you can model growth.

Your kids need to see how you handle failure even more than how you handle success. If you make a mistake, you need to own up to it and ask forgiveness if the situation calls for it. If you don't model how to deal with our own fleshly responses, how are they going to own up to their mistakes and resolve them biblically?

One Sunday morning my daughter wasn't ready when I wanted to leave for church. I fumed about it until I exploded with anger. After the service I was about to say grace before a meal when I felt the convicting hand of God weighing heavily upon me. I stopped and asked my family to forgive me for my outburst of anger. I didn't confess my daughter's tardiness because it wasn't my responsibility. Nor did I ask their forgiveness in hopes that she would own up to her tardiness. I asked their forgiveness because my outburst of anger was a deed of the flesh. I had to ask forgiveness to be right with God myself.

You never lose esteem in your child's eyes when you do what God requires you to do. You gain esteem because you are an honest person, and in the process you are modeling what they need to do when they blow it. Modeling is what establishes our credibility to "bring them up in the discipline and instruction of the Lord" (Ephesians 6:4).

ESTABLISHING YOUR CHILD'S SPIRITUAL IDENTITY

Your primary responsibility as a parent is to lead your child to Christ and help him establish his identity in Christ. When does this happen? To answer this, we need to review briefly the process of childhood development.

When a child comes into the world he is completely dependent on his earthly parents to feed him, change his dirty diapers, and provide shelter. Childhood and adolescence is the process of moving from total dependence as a

Age	Learns Sense of:	Key
Infancy (birth to 15 months)	Trust	Bonding, provide physical and emotional security
Toddler (1–3 years)	Autonomy	Shape the will and affirm personhood
Preschool (4–5 years)	Initiative	Promote creativity within limits
Grade School (6–11 years)	Accomplishment/ competence	Guidance and successful experiences
Junior High (12–15 years)	Identity vs. confusion	Confirmation, establish identity
H.S.–Young Adult (16–21 years)	Intimacy vs. isolation	Responsibility and becoming a friend

Figure 7a: Stages of development.

child to total independence as an adult. In the process of finding out who they are as individuals, children gradually move away from many of the people, thoughts, and ideas they have experienced through their parents and move toward the people, thoughts, and ideas which they have made their own.

Theorists like Erik Erikson (psycho-social development) and J. Piaget (cognitive development) have attempted to identify the stages of childhood development. They contend that normal maturity cannot be accomplished without a sequential progression through various stages of learning. Figure 7a is a combined view of their theories. The age ranges are approximate.

A newborn's identity is totally physical. But as he moves through the stages of his physical, emotional, and social development, his parents must help him establish his identity as a child of God. A child is capable of understanding God's love and protection and receiving Jesus Christ as Savior at a very early age. But understanding his spiritual identity is a process that takes place over the years of his childhood. It is the process of shifting his dependence from parents to God.

Notice from the chart that children wrestle with identity around age 12. Researchers of cognitive development say that most 12-year-olds can think as adults. They are capable of dealing with abstracts and understanding symbolism. This is significant when you remember that Jesus appeared out of obscurity at age 12. Furthermore, the Jewish bar mitzvah has been celebrated for centuries when a boy turns 12, the age at which Jews believe that a boy becomes a man.

As Figure 7b illustrates (see next page), I believe age 12 is the approximate time in a child's life when we should

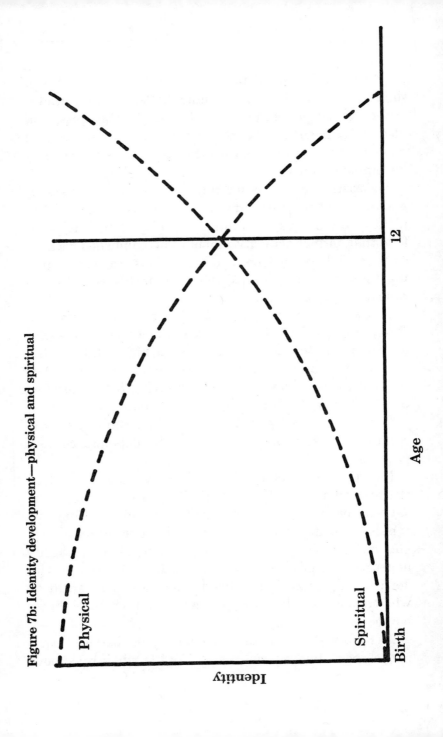

Figure 7b: Identity development—physical and spiritual

help him establish his spiritual identity. Children in liturgical churches have historically been confirmed on or near age 12. Possibly one of the greatest failures of the evangelical church is overlooking the need for confirmation when their faith is grounded in the truth of God's Word and their identity is established in Christ.

Evangelicals have tended to minimize junior high ministry and focus on high school. High school is too late for some kids to be challenged with their spiritual identity. Don't make that mistake with your children. You must begin early helping them understand who they are as children of God and what their identity means to them spiritually. Seeing themselves as God sees them is the most important perception your children will ever have. If they don't see themselves the way God sees them, they will suffer from a poor self-image. Spiritual identity is the most critical and foundational principle of the gospel. If your kids don't find their identity in Christ, they will find it in the world.

As you consider the importance of your spiritual identity and the spiritual identity of your children, meditate on these passages:

> The Spirit Himself bears witness with our spirit that we are children of God (Romans 8:16).

> For you are all sons of God through faith in Christ Jesus. For all of you who were baptized into Christ have clothed yourselves with Christ. There is neither Jew nor Greek, there is neither slave nor free man, there is neither male nor female; for you are all one in Christ (Galatians 3:26-29).

> And because you are sons, God has sent forth the Spirit of His Son into our hearts, crying, "Abba! Father!"

Therefore you are no longer a slave, but a son; and if a son, then an heir through God (Galatians 4:6,7).

But you are a chosen race, a royal priesthood, a holy nation, a people for God's own possession, that you may proclaim the excellencies of Him who has called you out of darkness into His marvelous light; for you once were not a people, but now you are the people of God; you had not received mercy, but now you have received mercy (1 Peter 2:9,10).

See how great a love the Father has bestowed upon us, that we should be called children of God; and such we are.... Beloved, now we are children of God, and it has not appeared as yet what we shall be. We know that, when He appears, we shall be like Him, because we shall see Him just as He is. And anyone who has this hope fixed on Him purifies himself, just as He is pure (1 John 3:1-3).

Mom and Dad, do you want your sons and daughters to purify themselves? Then find out who you are as a child of God, and help your children establish the same eternal relationship by discovering their identity in Him.

Chapter 8

STYLES
OF PARENTING

xxxxxxxxxxxxxxxxxxxxxxxxxxxxxxxxxxxxxxxxxxxxxx

S uppose you possessed the means to give your child the best. What kind of parent would you be? How would you raise him? What would you give him? What would you withhold from him? What would be your role in determining what your child should be and do?

The popular movie, *Dead Poets Society*, tells the story of a new teacher at an elite boys' boarding school who challenges his students to "seize the day" by discovering their own identity and potential. One young man is there because his father wants him to prepare for a career in medicine. "You can be whatever you want to be after you become a surgeon," the father declares. The young man dutifully tries to live up to his father's expectations.

The young man secretly tries out for and secures the lead role in a Shakespearean play in town against his father's will. The boy's opening night performance ends with a thunderous ovation. But his elation is soon dashed when he sees his father in the audience. Angered beyond reason, the father pulls him out of the play and the school. On his first night home the disillusioned young man takes his own life.

I (Neil) was involved in a similar parent-child conflict that, thankfully, had a much happier ending. Jill's parents were high-tech professionals and nominal Christians. Ever since she was three years old Jill had been given every opportunity to be the best. Driven by her parents to perfection, her grades were tops. Her parents wanted her to attend their alma mater and join her mother's sorority, but she wanted to attend a Christian college. Together they saw *Dead Poets Society*, and afterward her parents argued with her for hours that the father in the movie was right!

When Jill came to my office she was anorexic, struggling with her thought life, and had been cutting herself. In making a list of people she needed to forgive, her parents were right at the top. Her tears began slowly at first. "Lord, I forgive my father for never asking me what I wanted, for never even considering what I would like to do with my life." Then the flood gates opened, and she was able to find her freedom in Christ and begin a journey toward being what God wanted her to be. The voices stopped, the cutting stopped, and she was at peace in her mind. The spiritual component of her problem was resolved.

Soon the relational component was also resolved. Guided by her counselor, Jill reached a compromise with her parents. She attended their alma mater for one year, then transferred to a Christian school with their blessing.

We're not saying that misguided, overcontrolling parents cause their children to have spiritual problems. But parents who don't learn how to speak the truth in love and express their anger without sinning will give the devil an opportunity in their family (Ephesians 4:25-27). And if you and your children don't learn how to bear with each other and forgive one another in the close confinement of a family relationship, you will give Satan an advantage (Colossians 3:13; 2 Corinthians 2:10,11). And if you don't humble yourself, cast your parental anxieties on the Lord, and adopt an alert and sober spirit, you may be devoured by your adversary, the devil (1 Peter 5:8).

WHAT KIND OF PARENT ARE YOU?

I have no doubt that the father in *Dead Poets Society* cared for his son and wanted the best for him. Even Jill's parents would reject the accusation that they didn't love their daughter. Most Christian parents would do the right thing if they were sure what the right thing was. But what does a good parent do? What kind of parent minimizes the opportunities for satanic seduction in the family? Should you try to control your children? Is loving them the same as controlling them? Is controlling them the same as disciplining them?

Several years ago research was conducted to determine which parenting styles produced which kind of children.[1] The study solicited responses from hundreds of high school juniors and seniors throughout the United States. The questions were designed to reveal what kind of parents produced the following:

1. Children who have a good self-image and are happy being who they are.

2. Children who conform to the authority of others and have the capacity to get along with their teachers and other authority figures.

3. Children who follow the religious beliefs of their parents, attend the church of their parents, and are likely to continue to do so.

4. Children who identify with the counter-culture, rebelling against the norms of society.

Parents Who Control and Support

The research revealed the two most powerful influences in parenting: control and support. Parental control was defined as the ability to manage a child's behavior. Obviously there are many ways to control behavior. You can coerce your kids through intimidation, verbally batter them into submission, lay a guilt trip on them, or firmly establish boundaries and provide choices.

Parental support was defined as the ability to make a child feel loved. You need to do more than simply tell your child that you love him in order to help him feel loved. You must be physically and emotionally available in such a way that your child *knows* that you love him. Your love comes across in the way you communicate with and touch your child throughout the day. Communication is talking *with* your child, not just talking *to* him. Touching is holding, hugging, and kissing your child, not just bumping into him once in awhile.

Considering the two primary dimensions of control and support, there are four distinct parenting styles, as illustrated in Figure 8a.

The *permissive* parent offers high support and low control. This parent has the ability to make the child feel loved but makes little effort to control his behavior.

The *neglectful* parent provides low control and low support. This parent leaves the child alone, ignoring his responsibility to love the child and control his behavior.

The *authoritarian* parent provides high control and low support. This parent makes little attempt to love the child but works hard to control his behavior.

The *authoritative* parent offers high control and high support. This parent is able to make a child feel loved while adequately controlling his behavior.

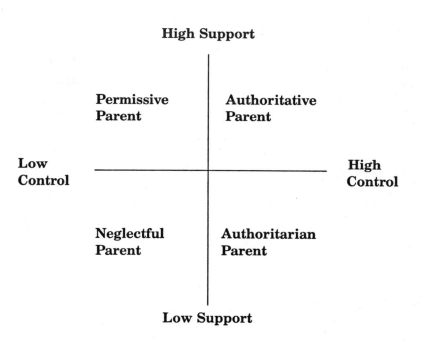

Figure 8a: Parental style types.

Which style do you think produces the best results? Figure 8b (on page 132) reveals how each parenting style ranks in the four desired categories: high sense of self-worth (SW), conform to authority (CTA), accept parents' religion (APR), rebel against society (REB).

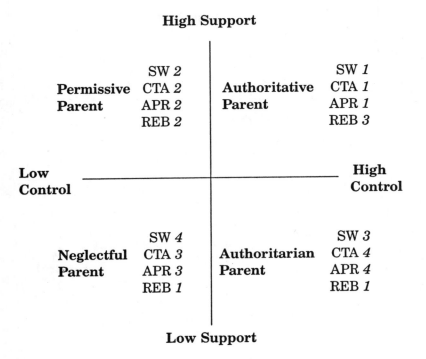

Figure 8b: Parenting style effectiveness.

As you can see from Figure 8b, the high control, high support style of the *authoritative* parent produced the most desirable results. Their children ranked first in self-worth, conforming to authority, and accepting parents' religion, and last in rebellion against society.

You may be surprised to discover that the *permissive* parent ranked second across the board in the four categories. The *neglectful* parent and *authoritarian* parent tied for the dubious distinction of raising the children most likely to rebel against the establishment. And they shared third and fourth place in the other categories.

Let's take another look, this time from the child's perspective. In his mind your child is continually asking two questions: "Can I get my own way?" and "Am I loved?" Figure 8c illustrates how each of the four parenting styles answer these questions and what these answers tend to produce in the child.

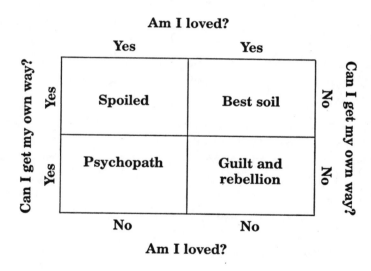

Figure 8c: Parental style from child's perspective.

The *permissive* parent answers yes to both questions. The child realizes he is loved, but he also discovers he can to do what he wants. This high support, low control parental response tends to result in a spoiled child.

The *neglectful* parent says, "No, I don't love you" and "Yes, you can do whatever you want." This low support, low control parental response is the most dangerous of all, creating a psychopathic mentality in the child.

The *authoritarian* parent answers no to both questions. The child feels trapped because he is overcontrolled and underloved. This high control, low support parental response results in guilt and rebellion in the child.

The *authoritative* parent assures the child that he is loved but warns him that he can't get his own way. This high control, high support parental response provides the best soil for positive parent-child relationships and productive lives.

It is obvious that parents who maintain firm discipline while demonstrating genuine love will have generally well-adjusted children. We believe common sense offers the same conclusion. Furthermore, the high ranking of the *permissive* parent indicates that loving your child is more important than controlling him. The tragedy is that most parents resort to an authoritarian style when problems begin to surface. When push comes to shove, many parents stop loving and start controlling. But according to this study, that's the worst parenting style.

The Need to Control

More times than not, this need to control our children comes from the false belief that our identity and self-worth derives from how well our children behave. Think it through: If your self-worth comes from something outside yourself, your natural tendency is to control the people and factors on which your worth is based. Look at sick dictators like Adolf Hitler and Saddam Hussein who control their subjects through ruthless force and intimidation. But there is no one more insecure than a controller, because he labors under the false belief that the external affairs of this world are determining who he is, not God and his response to Him. The fruit of the Spirit is self-control (Galatians 5:23), not child- or spouse-control.

If your identity is in Christ and your heart is set on being the person God wants you to be, nobody can block that goal but you. "But what if my child rebels?" you ask. Your child can't stop you from being the father or mother God wants you to be. Only you can do that. In reality, during a crisis of rebellion your child and your spouse need you to be the parent God wants you to be more than ever.

Here's the point: You may not always be able to control your child, but based on your position and character in Christ you can always love him. Loving your child is dependent only on you and your response to God. Controlling him is somewhat dependent on the cooperation of your child. Your identity and security in Christ does not depend on things you have no right or ability to control.

LEARNING TO LOVE YOUR CHILD

The Bible admonishes older women to encourage young women to love their husbands and their children (Titus 2:4). For many people, loving their children is a nebulous concept. What does it mean to love our children? Fortunately, *agape* love is very clearly defined in the Scriptures. Love is the highest of character attainments: "The goal of our instruction is love from a pure heart and a good conscience and a sincere faith" (1 Timothy 1:5). Love is the fruit of the Spirit (Galatians 5:22), the means by which a true disciple of Christ is identified (John 13:35). The attention given to love in passages such as 1 Corinthians 13 and 1 John 4 reveals its importance to God in our interpersonal relationships, of which the family is primary.

Agape love is not dependent on the person being loved, but on the lover. You like your child because of who he is; but you love him because of who *you* are. God loves us not because we are lovable but because God is love. If it was any other way God's love would be conditional. If you performed better would God love you more? Of course not. Real love is not based on performance.

If you say you don't love your child, you have said more about yourself than about your child. Specifically, you're saying that you haven't attained the maturity to love him unconditionally (Luke 6:32). The grace of God enables you to love your child in a way that the parent without Christ cannot. God doesn't command you to like your child, because you can't order your emotions to respond. But He does instruct you to love your child. You can always choose to do the loving thing and trust that your feelings will follow in time.

Loving the Difficult Child

Love can't be separated from action. Jesus said, "If you love Me, you will keep My commandments" (John 14:15). If you say you love your child but don't follow through with loving words and deeds, you are contradicting yourself. It is the presence of God in our lives that enables us to love our children, even when they are difficult to love.

A missionary couple stopped by my office to talk about their misbehaving five-year-old daughter. The father lamented, "Neil, Sarah is so difficult to handle that we have to drop her off at my parents' home every other weekend so that we can get away. We want to love Sarah, and we are going to choose to do that. But she is so difficult to be around that there are times we just hate her! She is ruining our home, and the pressure on our marriage is threatening to pull us apart." Can you hear the pain and frustration in these words? Can you imagine the mixed feelings these parents must have?

I encouraged them to ask Sarah what was going on in her mind when she acted belligerently. They seemed a little skeptical, but they agreed to try. To their surprise Sarah admitted to receiving all kinds of bizarre thoughts as well as having frightening experiences in her room. The parents made an appointment with me and brought Sarah with them. Together we took a stand against the enemy. I heard from the parents six months later that Sarah was living a "normal" life.

A father pulled me aside after a speaking engagement. "Neil, I have a problem with my 14-year-old daughter, Mindy," he began. "There's a barrier between us to the point that we can hardly talk. What should I do?" I suggested that he read my book, *The Bondage Breaker*, to become informed enough to help her.

As he was reading the book at home, Mindy asked him what he was reading. As he explained to her the material about the battle for the mind, she poured out her own story of mental assault. Finally knowing the true nature of her problem he was able to work with her toward resolving her conflict and their differences.

When an emotional barrier has been erected between parent and child, it is almost impossible for the parent to resolve the spiritual conflict. If the problem persists for any period of time, the child will summarily reject all authority figures. Your child may be difficult to like at this point, but you must love him enough to become informed and seek qualified help.

Meeting Your Child's Needs

When love is used as a verb in the Bible it requires the lover to meet the needs of the one being loved. Love must be given away. God so loved the world that He gave (John 3:16). The corollary to John 3:16 is 1 John 3:16-18: "We know love by this, that He laid down His life for us; and we ought to lay down our lives for the brethren. But whoever has the world's goods, and beholds his brother in need and closes his heart against him, how does the love of God abide in him? Little children, let us not love with word or with tongue, but in deed and truth."

The essence of love is meeting needs, and our most important assignment from God is to meet the needs of those who are closest to us: "If any one does not provide for his own, and especially for those of his household, he has denied the faith, and is worse than an unbeliever" (1 Timothy 5:8). We tend to use the people close to us while meeting the needs of those who aren't even in the family. So the busy homemaker is out resolving everybody else's child-rearing problems but her own. The pastor is available to everybody but his wife and children. And the executive will work overtime to solve company problems while ignoring needs at home.

Take an inventory of your child's needs. We're not talking about external needs like clothing, education, and food. We're talking about gut-level needs that determine his sense of identity and belonging. When was the last time you hugged your child and told him you loved him? Have you noticed his good character qualities and pointed them out to him? If all you ever point out is physical qualities or achievements, your child will base his worth on how well he performs and looks instead of developing character. Do you regularly reinforce good behavior, or do you only notice the poor behavior? When your child does something nice do you thank him? Does your child know that he is loved and valued from the way you talk to him?

Learning to Control Behavior

A child begins to seek his identity and assert his independence as he approaches the age of 12. The average parent is usually somewhat permissive until then, but he starts to panic when the child assumes his own identity and starts pulling away. By the time the child reaches 14 everything flies apart. Fearing the worst, the parent becomes authoritarian by tightening the screws of discipline and restricting the child's activities. A power struggle ensues with predictable results. The child bolts, and the parent calls for advice.

The problem of the rebellious, stubborn, disobedient child was easily resolved in the Old Testament: The child was stoned by the men of the city (Deuteronomy 21:18-21). Sometimes we wish discipline was that simple! Yet this passage helps us understand that even decent parents who try to be good disciplinarians sometimes have stubborn and rebellious children. Why? Because you aren't the only influence in your child's life. And by the time he enters school you are no longer even the predominant influence. But during the formative years from birth to five, you have your greatest influence. Your most important task during that period (especially around ages two and three) is to break the child's will without breaking his spirit. It is then that you must establish boundaries of behavior that are progressively expanded until the child is on his own.

A Spiritual Solution to the Spiritual Problem

If you fail to control the child during his early years, problems won't usually show up until he hits the age of identity, around 12. Most parents respond at this time by trying to control the child. But remember: The authoritarian parent is most likely to produce a rebel. "But we have to reprove rebellious kids, don't we?" you ask. Actually, the Bible tells us *not* to reprove a scoffer (Proverbs 9:7-9). Why? Because a rebellious attitude is a spiritual problem, and it needs a spiritual solution.

Take the example of Saul, the first king of Israel, who rebelled against God by doing his own thing, making his own rules, and worshiping the way he wanted to. God sent a prophet to confront him. Part of the prophet's stinging rebuke was, "Rebellion is as the sin of divination [witchcraft], and insubordination is as iniquity and idolatry" (1 Samuel 15:23). As a result of Saul's disobedience, "an evil spirit from the Lord terrorized him" (1 Samuel 16:14).

God can use any means He chooses to discipline His children. Even Satan and his evil spirits can be an instrument in the hands of God. In the case of blatant immorality, Paul said, "I have decided to deliver such a one to Satan for the destruction of his flesh, that his spirit may be saved in the day of the Lord Jesus" (1 Corinthians 5:5). We're not suggesting that you turn your child over to Satan. But willful disobedience usually cannot be dealt with by human reasoning. Prayer is our weapon for bringing down the strongholds raised up against the knowledge of God (2 Corinthians 10:3-5). We will further discuss the role of prayer in the home in Chapter 12.

Nor are we saying that you shouldn't rebuke your child. On the contrary, you must rebuke him, but you must do it in love and start early. God spoke to Samuel regarding Eli's failure to rebuke his sons, "I will carry out against Eli all that I have spoken concerning his house, from beginning to end. For I have told him that I am about to judge his house forever for the iniquity which he knew, because his sons brought a curse on themselves and he did not rebuke them" (1 Samuel 3:12,13). Eli was an effective priest but a defective parent.

Guidelines for the Problem Child

So what should you do if you have a rebellious child at home? Follow this simple logic. Is the Holy Spirit controlling your child when he is rebelling? Absolutely not! Then should you let that child control you or your family? No! One of the primary functions of a spiritual leader in the home is to ensure that the Spirit of God is ruling the household. And shepherding your flock means that you must assume responsibility for driving off the spiritual wolves.

Years ago when I was a youth pastor, I caught two girls from our church smoking in the youth lounge. Sherrie and Tannis both knew that the lounge was off limits without a supervisor. So I told them that they were suspended from all youth social activities and summer camp until they took the initiative to come in with their parents.

Three weeks passed before Sherrie's parents called me: "Neil, we need to set up an appointment." When they came in Sherrie was visibly upset and repentant. I assured her parents that I had no other agenda than to have Sherrie own up to her behavior with them. Since she did, I told them that Sherrie was free to participate with the youth group in any way they saw fit. Sherrie's parents later told me how much they appreciated the action I took. It was a turning point in Sherrie's life.

Tannis obviously heard from Sherrie that confession wasn't too hard, so Tannis told her parents about the incident, and they came in to see me. But Tannis just sat and glared at me. I asked her to step outside while I talked to her parents. I said, "I don't see any signs of remorse or repentance in Tannis. I suggest that the restriction remain in place." They reluctantly agreed to my suggestion.

Several weeks went by before Tannis came to me and offered a lame confession. It was obvious to me that she just wanted to go to camp, but I had no recourse but to accept her apology. To do less would be to judge her.

On the first night of camp Tannis acted up. I called her into the camp office and said that I was not going to allow her to destroy the camp for the other 125 students that were there. I said, "Tomorrow morning you will be raking rocks while the rest are meeting." I wasn't mad at her, and I made sure she knew I wasn't. I also assured Tannis that I wasn't just protecting the group from her, but I was disciplining her in love for her own good. We can't overstate the importance of not violating the fruit of the Spirit when disciplining a child. You are responsible for maintaining self-control and confronting the child in love.

Before the confrontation was over, I assured Tannis that there would be no warnings. If I had to talk to her again for disciplinary reasons it would be to arrange for her parents

to come pick her up. I'm glad for her sake that I never had
to confront her again.

Don't allow a discipline problem to go unchecked until
you lose control and lash out in anger. That's a deed of the
flesh not a fruit of the Spirit. You must take action before
you lose self-control, and the best way to do that is not to
give any warnings. Act decisively and swiftly in love.
Tannis' parents later shared with me that I was one of the
first youth leaders to hold my ground with Tannis without
losing self-control.

In Chapter 10 we will deal with discipline in greater
detail. But at this point let us offer several general guidelines for responding to a difficult child.

*1. Determine if the behavior is rebellious or merely child-
ish.* I was teaching a young marrieds' class when my son
was only two. Five minutes before I was to start my class, a
frustrated woman entered the room and got my attention.
"Neil, your son is having a temper tantrum behind the
piano in the two-year-old department!" I followed her to
the classroom and went behind the piano. Within 30 seconds Karl came out, said something to the teacher, and
that was that.

Later she asked me what I did to him. I gave her this
same explanation. I wanted to find out if he was defiantly
determined to stay behind that piano and show who was
strongest or if he was just stuck behind the piano, didn't
know how to get out, and was too embarrassed to ask. So I
asked him, "Karl, are you stuck back here and don't know
how to get out?"

"Yeah," he answered, sniffling.

I said, "You know the teacher is embarrassed too. If you
just went over to the teacher and said you were sorry that it
happened, everything would be all right."

"It would?"

"Yes, Karl. Can you do that?"

"Yeah!" He did, and it was all over.

2. Don't let the problem child come between you and your spouse. Satan designs to use a problem situation to put you and your spouse at odds with each other. Jesus said, "A house divided against itself falls" (Luke 11:17). Many times I have said to parents, "Don't let this pull you apart." Inevitably they glance at each other, because that's precisely what's been going on.

"If you would have been more firm with her, this wouldn't have happened," one blames.

"It's because you didn't set the standard by having family devotions every night," the other retorts.

Or if they did have devotions, "You just read to them, you never communicate with them!"

"If you were home more often, I'd have more time to communicate with them."

There may be a grain of truth in every statement above. But it's history, and tearing each other down will only make the problem worse. You must be united in order to survive the crisis. Character-bashing is from the pit.

3. Don't compromise your godly standards or beliefs. Many parents are intimidated by a child's threats or find it easier to give in to a temper tantrum than not to. But you cannot let a rebellious child rule the home. It takes an iron will and the grace of God to stand your ground and not let your child control you. Sad are the children whose parents let them rule the roost.

Even sadder are the children whose parents rule without love. If you manage to control through loveless intimidation and force, your child will be emotionally crippled.

Proverbs 27:22 says: "You can't separate a rebel from his foolishness though you crush him to powder" (TLB).

4. Accept the fact that you may not be able to control your child when he is out of your presence. When your child leaves your home, he leaves with his own values, beliefs, and personal agenda. This is the first half of the prodigal son story (Luke 15:11-32). The prodigal son wanted to do his own thing, so his father let him. I don't think the father would have let the boy rule in his home, but he did let him go. We don't like to see our children fail or make mistakes like that. When they do, we are too quick to rescue them from the natural consequences of their actions.

The father in the story welcomed his son home after the boy came to his senses. His repentance was complete: "Father, I have sinned against heaven and in your sight; I am no longer worthy to be called your son" (verse 21). The critical insight we need is offered by the father: "This son of mine was dead, and has come to life again" (verse 24). When your child is out of your sight, only God can bring him to his senses, bring him home, and give him life.

5. Pray. You can't go everywhere your child goes, but God can. He is the child's Father, and He is fully capable of protecting him.

Barbara Johnson is the founder of Spatula Ministries and author of *Where Does a Mother Go to Resign?* (Bethany House Publishers). This dear lady has buried two sons and witnessed the miracle healing of her husband from a near-fatal car accident. But her hardest trial was discovering that her beloved third son was struggling with homosexuality. Months of dark depression were lifted in one day when she realized that her son belonged to God, so she gave her boy to Him. For 11 years she didn't hear from him.

Then one day he called and said he had a Mother's Day present for her. He had come back to the Lord!

God is in control. When you pray you release Him to do what only He can do in your child's life. And when you pray, He can mold your parenting style so you can do what He has called you to do in raising your child.

Chapter 9

CAN YOUR CHILD TALK TO YOU?

xxxxxxxxxxxxxxxxxxxxxxxxxxxxxxxxxxxxxxxxxxxxxxxxxxxxxxxxxxxxx

A desperate mother of three stopped by my office needing a spiritual transfusion. "I can't get a handle on my problems, Neil," Ruth complained. "I know my children are struggling at school, but they won't share it with me. Why won't they talk to me?"

"Do you really want to know, Ruth?"

"Of course!"

"They probably don't feel they can trust you," I responded.

"What do you mean they can't trust me? I'm their mother!"

"Let me illustrate," I said. "Suppose your 15-year-old daughter came home one day and said that her best friend was taking drugs. What would you say to her?"

Ruth paused for a moment, then said, "I'd probably tell her to find another friend."

"Exactly! And that's why she doesn't share that kind of information with you."

"Well, what would you say?" Ruth asked, rather put out.

"I don't think I would respond that way; at least I hope I wouldn't."

Like a lot of parents, Ruth was in the habit of reacting to
her kids before she had a clue about what was really going
on. Two or three reactions like this from you and your child
is ready to clam up forever. Whenever your child tells you
about "my friend's problem," there is a very good chance
that he's the one with the problem. He will drop little hints
about his "friend" to see your reaction. If you are hasty and
judgmental, you can bet he won't share any more. Wise
Solomon wrote: "He who gives an answer before he hears,
it is folly and shame to him" (Proverbs 18:13).

Clear, loving communication in your family is impera-
tive if you are going to foil Satan's attempt to seduce your
child. After all, if you don't listen when he tells you about
his school problems, he may not bother to tell you about his
evil thoughts. And if you criticize him when he admits his
mistakes, he won't want you to know about the terrifying
dark presence he experiences in his room at night. Faulty
communication doesn't necessarily cause spiritual problems in your child, but it can certainly block or delay the
resolution of those problems.

WHAT'S YOUR COMMUNICATION STYLE?

Lawrence Richards has provided a helpful explanation
of parent-child communication. Drawing from the work of
Ross Snyder, Richards characterized four levels of parental
response, as illustrated in Figure 9a (on page 147).[1]

The child in the boat is headed for certain disaster. He
obviously made a bad decision upstream. His parent will
respond in one of four ways.

The *advice-giver* is far removed from the emotional
crisis. He hollers, "Row harder! Why did you get into the

water in the first place? What a stupid kid! I told you not to do it. Didn't you read the warning signs?"

The *reassurer* is closer to the situation and responds, "You were a good kid. Your mother and I love you. Of the last three people who went over the falls, two survived. Good luck!"

The *understander* steps into the water and says, "Hey, the current is very strong here. You really are in trouble, aren't you? Let me see if I can get you some help."

But the *self-revealer* gets into the boat with the child and immediately starts paddling to safety.

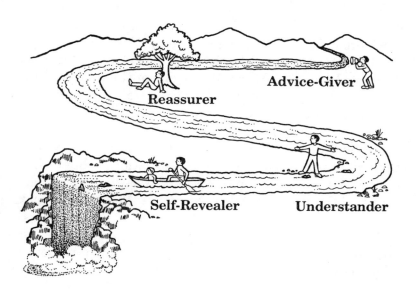

Figure 9a: Parent-child communication.

Here's another illustration. Suppose your child comes home from school with sorrow written all over his face. You ask him what's wrong, and he tells you that his best friend has rejected him. How would you respond?

If you are an *advice-giver* you might say something like, "I never did like that kid anyway. What did you do to make him reject you? Next time be more careful about choosing your friends. I think what you need to do is..."

If you are a *reassurer* you will probably wrap your arms around him and say, "Your mother and I love you. You're a good kid, and I know you will survive this crisis. You'll find another friend."

If you are an *understander* you might respond, "Hey, that hurts, doesn't it? Can we sit down and talk about it? Can you share with me what happened?"

But if you're a *self-revealer* you will give the child a hug and sit silently with him for a moment reflecting on a time you were rejected. Then you may respond, "Two years ago my best friend turned his back on me. I trusted him as much as I trusted anyone. It was one of the most painful experiences of my life. I sense you are going through the same thing I did."

We have asked hundreds of teenagers to identify how their parents respond in similar situations. Ninety-five percent identified their parents as *advice-givers*. Five percent said their parents were *reassurers*. Not one teenager identified his parents as *understanders* or *self-revealers*. We're not saying that you don't need to give advice and offer reassurance to your child. Nor is any one response appropriate in every situation. But a serious communication problem exists when kids report that their parents respond almost exclusively with advice-giving and reassurance.

My daughter Heidi and three of her friends were involved in an automobile accident that sent all four girls to the emergency unit at the hospital. Fortunately they all escaped serious injury. I was the first parent to arrive at the hospital, so I went to each of the girls and prayed with them.

The driver of the car was in hysterics. The nurse had her breathing into a paper bag because she was hyperventilating. "My dad is going to kill me," she said. I tried to assure her that he would be as relieved as I was that there were no serious injuries. I was wrong. He came in with both barrels blazing. Calling him an *advice-giver* would be kind.

I pulled him aside. "Were you ever involved in an accident when you were young?" I asked.

"Sure, I really raised Cain when I was young! That's why I'm so ticked off at her."

"My daughter is in the other room, and I'm just thankful that nothing serious happened," I responded. "Your daughter doesn't need you to be ticked off at her. She needs a father who can identify with what she is going through. You seem like someone who would understand since the same thing happened to you."

When your child is hurt or in trouble, he needs a *self-revealer* to get into the boat with him. If you don't adopt this communication style, your child may eventually be the victim of an even greater disaster.

A Parent Kids Can Talk To

Halfway through the semester in my class on pastoral counseling I ask each student to write on a blank sheet of paper the last thing he would want anyone to know about himself. They stare at me in disbelief, and the anxiety in the room rises to the rafters. They're thinking about the worst thing they could write, but they aren't about to put it on paper. Instead they are getting ready to write down something much less incriminating.

After I let them sweat for a few seconds I call a halt to the exercise. I really don't want them to write down their worst secret, but I do want them to feel the anxiety of facing that possibility. Can you imagine how some people feel as they approach a pastor or counselor knowing that if they are going to receive any help they will have to disclose what the real problem is? Do you remember how you felt as you approached your parents with a problem when you were young?

While my students breathe a sigh of relief, I ask, "What kind of person would you share your deepest, most painful secret with?" Here are some of the responses I receive:

Someone I could really trust.

An accepting person.

Someone with empathy.

Someone who could reciprocate.

A nonjudgmental person.

A person who understands me.

Someone who cares about me.

A person with wisdom.

After the list is complete I ask, "Will you purpose in your heart to be that kind of person to your friends and parishioners?" Your child is looking for the same kind of person to share his hurts and fears with. Will you purpose in your heart to be the kind of parent your daughter or son can come to and confide in?

COMMUNICATING
LOVE, TRUST, AND RESPECT

A woman who came to me for counseling spilled tons of messy details about her life. The next morning she called and said, "Neil, I feel terrible about sharing all that dirt about my life. What do you think of me?"

"I love you for it," I responded.

There was a brief pause. "Well, if that's the case, I have a lot more to tell you!"

The same is true with our kids. If we communicate judgment and criticism, they won't feel comfortable sharing their spiritual problems with us. But if they know we will respond with love, trust, and respect for them no matter what they tell us, they will open up like flowers in the sunshine.

"I Love You"

There are four concepts we deal with as parents in communicating with our children: authority, accountability, affirmation, and acceptance. We usually line them up this way:

We exert our parental authority over them.

We demand that they be accountable to us.

When they respond to our authority and comply by being accountable, we affirm them.

When they put together a positive track record of affirmative behaviors, we convey our love and acceptance.

The reason we have such difficulty communicating with our children is that we have it all backward. Look at God's approach to us as His children. At which end of the list does our Heavenly Father start? Does He come to us as the great authority figure demanding accountability? When you read the Gospels do you ever hear Jesus saying, "You'd better listen to Me, because I'm God!"? No, God starts by expressing His love and acceptance (John 3:16; Romans 5:8).

Even the great apostle Paul approached his flock with acceptance. He wrote to the Thessalonian church:

> For we never came with flattering speech, as you know, nor with a pretext for greed—God is witness— nor did we seek glory from men, either from you or from others, even though as apostles of Christ we might have asserted our authority. But we proved to be gentle among you, as a nursing mother tenderly cares for her own children. Having thus a fond affection for you, we were well-pleased to impart to you not only the gospel of God but also our own lives, because you had become very dear to us (1 Thessalonians 2:5-8).

Paul started with acceptance. He shared his life. He earned the right to be heard, and so must we. Our children won't care how much we know until they know how much we care. Paul instructs us to "accept one another, just as Christ also accepted us to the glory of God" (Romans 15:7). When your child shares something personal with you, what is he looking for initially? Not a lecture, not a list of rules he must obey, but acceptance and affirmation. "Tell me I'm all right," he begs. "Give me some love and hope."

When you know that you are unconditionally loved and

accepted by God and affirmed in your identity as His child, you voluntarily submit to His authority and hold yourself accountable to Him. And when you are accepted and affirmed by those in authority over you (employer, pastor, etc.), you have no problem being accountable to their authority. Similarly, when your child knows that you love him and accept him regardless of his failures, he will feel safe sharing his problems with you and responding to the direction you give.

Rules without relationship lead to rebellion. Loving relationships seldom need rules to regulate behavior. Children who know they are loved are free to be themselves, free to grow, and free to be the person God wants them to be.

A well-known pastor named Charlie tells this story about himself. When Charlie was first married there were some shady parts of his past that he hadn't told his wife about. Fearing that she would find out about his past eventually, he decided to confess everything before she heard from someone else. Unable to tell her face to face, he wrote down his confession and solemnly read it to her.

"What do you think?" he asked, unable to look up at her.

"Charlie, there isn't anything you could share with me that just by having you share it wouldn't cause me to love you more." That's the kind of loving acceptance we need to express to our children.

Would you react as this woman did if your child shared with you that he was hearing voices or struggling with evil thoughts? Our culture has communicated that anyone with these symptoms is having mental problems. Most of the people who come to me for help have been in counseling for years. In most cases they have never shared with their counselors the spiritual battle for their minds. They will talk about the abuses they've suffered and their family struggles but not the mental battle. Why not? Because they don't trust anyone with that information. They're already afraid they are going crazy. And they fear that their counselors won't believe them anyway. This fear is well-founded. I once listened to a tape of counselors discussing their clients. They were laughing about the clients who were desperate enough to share what the voices in their heads were saying. I could have cried!

There are two reasons why the battle for the mind remains a private nightmare for kids as well as adults. First, they don't know who to trust. One of my students put it well: "I've always been told that I have an overactive imagination. I tried to share once in a church group the turmoil going on in my mind. People sucked in their breath, and someone changed the subject. I could have died. I learned very quickly that this type of problem can't be shared in our churches."

You can't read your child's mind, so if he doesn't trust you, his problem will remain hidden. You must gain your child's trust if you are going to help him resolve his spiritual conflicts.

Second, children are afraid. The enemy grips people with terrible fear. I was stalled in dealing with a young girl, knowing that she wasn't sharing with me what was going on in her mind. I said, "You're not sharing everything with me, are you? You're being intimidated by voices warning you not to divulge certain information—probably threatening to harm you when you get home." She nodded.

"Satan's lies are his way of intimidating you to keep you from resolving your problems," I said. "When you gain your freedom in Christ, you will be free at home as well."

"How can I be sure of that?" she asked.

"Trust me!" I urged. Do you see how the enemy uses fear and lack of trust to keep people in bondage?

"I Trust You"

Most parents are blind to a child's lack of trust because they are so caught up in not trusting their child. "How can I ever trust my child?" they ask. "He is totally untrustworthy!" The truth of the matter is that we don't have a choice. We have to trust them. We can't follow them around for the rest of their lives. If we're going to help our children grow, develop, and walk in freedom, we must communicate our trust in them.

When I was 14 years old my family moved off the farm in Minnesota where I was born. But I never adjusted to our new home in Arizona. When I was only 15 my parents let me take a bus back to Minnesota to work on the farm for the summer. The following summer I drove an old Studebaker back to Minnesota by myself. (I wonder how many parents would let their 16-year-old child do that today?) The family I stayed with asked if I would like to live with them and finish high school in Minnesota. To my great joy my parents said it was okay.

Shortly thereafter I saw a letter from my mother written to the couple I was staying with. I believe it was left out for me to see. In the letter my mother said, "Take care of Neil; he is my favorite." I believe that every child in our family is Mom's favorite, and I believe she was clever enough to arrange the whole adventure.

What impact did my parents' trust have on me? I never wanted to do anything to lose their trust. Their trust in me was a great driving force in my life and the greatest gift they ever gave me. Next to the Holy Spirit in me, that trust has been the greatest deterrent to immorality. Even years later when I was in the military and thousands of miles from home, I didn't want to lose their trust.

When you effectively communicate your love, trust, and respect to your child, he will learn to value these qualities so much that he will never intentionally do anything to lose them. Then when he is introduced to Christ, he will also value His love, trust, and respect. "But my child isn't trustworthy," you say. Neither are you completely trustworthy. Yet God has entrusted you with the gospel. That gives you something to live up to. What can you possibly gain by communicating anything less than your trust in your child?

Paul wrote to the church at Corinth: "I rejoice that in everything I have confidence in you" (2 Corinthians 7:16). Come on, Paul, the church at Corinth? Try the church in Rome or maybe in Ephesus. They were strong. But Corinth was a messed up place. Is Paul's statement a bunch of psychological hype? No, I don't think so. Paul's confidence was in the Lord, and he knew that the work God had begun in the Corinthian believers would be completed. Under the inspiration of God he also knew that expressing belief and confidence in them was foundational for building them up.

It is difficult to estimate the damage done by saying to a child:

You'll never amount to anything.

You can't do anything right, can you?

Why can't you be like him?

You're no son of mine!

I'm not going to invest any more money in you.

You're just like all the other kids.

Why not communicate your trust instead and give your child something to live up to? See the potential, not the problems.

Imagine how Peter felt when Jesus looked at him and said, "You are Simon the son of John; you shall be called Cephas (which translated means Peter [or rock])" (John 1:42). Peter went on about his business of fishing. Sometime later Jesus called him to be a disciple. After Peter's great confession that Jesus was the Christ, Jesus said to him, "You are Peter, and upon this rock I will build My church" (Matthew 16:18). What confidence Jesus expressed in a smelly, uneducated fisherman who would later deny Him three times!

Would you have chosen Peter and expressed confidence in him? Would you have stuck with Peter after he betrayed you? Jesus did, and He is sticking with you, too. He has entrusted you with His message, gifted you to serve, and blessed you with children. Are you trustworthy? Not completely. But His trust sure gives you something to live up to, doesn't it? Your trust in your child can do the same for him.

"I Respect You"

The flip side of trusting our children is respecting them. They are little adults created in the image of God. Talk to them with the same sense of respect you would extend to an adult.

After hearing me give a series on training children, a good friend of mine decided that he would ask his son how he could show him more respect. His son scribbled these lines on a sheet of paper. His simple words are excellent advice for all parents.

1. Walk around me, don't walk over me.

2. When we are at other houses, don't get mad and make dirty faces at me. Be happy and make happy faces.

3. Don't sit on your seat and watch TV, like football games. Go to the park or school and play games.

4. Or stay home and play games.

5. Spend more time with me and we will be better than before.

COMMUNICATING DURING CONFLICT

At no time does our ability or inability to communicate with our children reveal itself more than during conflict. The level of your regard for your family relationships and your drive to achieve will play a major role in determining how you communicate during conflicts, as illustrated in Figure 9b.

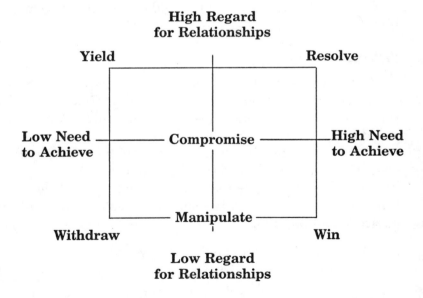

Figure 9b: Family relationships levels.

The parent with a low regard for relationships and a high need to achieve wants to *win* during conflict. Low regard for relationships also allows for manipulation in the quest to win the conflict.

The parent with a low regard for relationships and a low need to achieve will probably *withdraw* from conflict.

The parent with a high regard for relationships and a low need to achieve is likely to *yield* during conflict.

The parent with a high regard for relationships and a high need to achieve will work to *resolve* conflict.

The parent who lives in the middle ground between these fields will seek *compromise* in conflicts.

Chances are good that you learned your method of handling conflict from one or both of your parents. Children either adopt or react against what their parents model in the home. As you study the diagram, answer the following questions:

1. How do (did) your father and mother respond to conflict?

2. With which parent do (did) you communicate better?

3. How do you respond to conflict?

4. Which parent are you most like?

5. Is your style of conflict response opposite to one or both of your parents?

6. Which styles best facilitate communication?

7. Which styles reflect personal insecurity?

8. Which issue is more important to you: regard for relationships or the need to achieve?

Many parents find that their need to achieve in conflicts with their children is greater than their regard for relationships. Why is winning so important to us? Why must we always be right? The person who is driven to win, to be right, or to be first is insecure. Insecure people are driven to perform. The styles of conflict response on the lower half of the diagram reflect insecurity.

Security comes from relationships, not achievements. A secure person is a person who is comfortable with himself and others. It is easy to communicate with a secure person, but you always end up arguing with a driven person. Would you rather be a lover or an achiever? Which would you prefer your children to be?

Relationships are more important than achievements to God. Jesus declared that the two greatest commandments are to love God and love people (Matthew 22:36-40). The purpose of the Word of God is to govern our relationships with God and man. If our achievements in life don't enhance our relationships with God, our spouse and children, and others, then we are not fulfilling God's commandments.

Is there ever a time when we need to win in conflicts with our children? Yes, we need to stand our ground on moral issues. But we never have the right to violate the fruit of the Spirit in doing so. If what you do can't be done in love and self-control, then maybe it's better left undone. And remember: Your authority does not increase with the volume of your voice. When you resort to shouting in conflict you are reacting in the flesh. You have lost control of the only person you can control: yourself.

I remember one difficult evening when my daughter was sick but still wanted to go to the beach with her friends even though we said no. During the conflict she completely lost control and accused me of keeping her from having any fun. She called me a lousy parent and every other name she could think of. I continued to stand my ground without raising my voice. I had to physically stand in her way to keep her from leaving. Her friends arrived, and I explained my decision. She and her friends talked for a long time, then she came out and apologized for her behavior.

In power struggles like these we must win for the sake of our children. But we only win if we maintain our walk with God and fulfill our responsibility as parents. Remember, you may not always be able to control your child, but you can always love him. Your relationship with him is more important than anything you achieve.

Two significant events in my life brought into clear focus the priority of relationships over achievement. Before being called into the ministry I worked as an aerospace engineer on the Apollo program. I will never forget the day the lunar lander touched down on the moon. This bold headline dominated the front page of the *Minneapolis Star*: "Neil Armstrong Lands on the Moon." It was an achievement I was proud to be part of.

But the really big news came months earlier on page 7 in the third section: "Heidi Jo Anderson, born to Mr. and Mrs. Neil Anderson, Northwestern Hospital, March 12, 1969." That may not sound like big news to you, but it was to us. Heidi totally took over my den and captured an entire shelf in the refrigerator. She altered our sleeping pattern and restricted our social calendar. But she was ours to hold, to hug, and to care for.

What does God care about moon-shots? They are deeds to be outdone. Somebody will always come along and do it better, faster, and higher. What God cares about is little people like Heidi Jo, because they will be with Him forever.

Chapter 10

SHAPING YOUR CHILD
TO BE FREE

XXXXXXXXXXXXXXXXXXXXXXXXXXXXXXXXXXXXXXXXXXXXXXXXXXXXXXXXXXXXXXXXXXXXX

You only have one shot at raising your children, and you really want to do a good job. You know that discipline is a large part of parenting, but which method should you use: the one your parents used on you? the one preached by your pastor? the one taught at that parenting seminar you attended? the one espoused by your favorite Christian author?

To illustrate the complexity of the discipline problem, check whether you agree or disagree with the following statements:

Agree   **Disagree**

_____   _____   1. The best way to handle a child's temper tantrum is to ignore it.

_____   _____   2. When making rules, if a child's opinion is better than the parents', the parents should change their mind.

_____   _____   3. Spanking is the biblical way to discipline, and all children benefit from it.

_____ _____ 4. A four-year-old child who wets his bed should change his own sheets.

_____ _____ 5. Angry children should not be allowed to say "I hate you" to their parents.

_____ _____ 6. Money is an effective reward to get children to do their chores.

_____ _____ 7. Children are born with a sin nature, and parents should discipline them to eliminate this natural tendency.

_____ _____ 8. A parent should count to five to give a child time to obey.

_____ _____ 9. Some preschool children just will not stay in bed in the evening and should not be forced to do so.

_____ _____ 10. If it is wrong for a child to watch a television program, it is also wrong for his parents to watch it.

Groups of Christian parents are typically split down the middle on each of these statements. They all read the same Bible and have usually been exposed to the same Christian literature. But they still come up with different opinions. Christian parents know they need to discipline their children, but different children require different styles of discipline.

What does discipline have to do with the satanic seduction of our children? As with the other attitudes and skills for parents we have discussed, a child's spiritual problems are not the direct result of a parent's struggle to discipline him. But if you are not seeking to follow scriptural guidelines for shaping your child through discipline, you may be opening windows of opportunity for Satan, who is intent on capturing him and molding him for his own purposes.

WHAT IS DISCIPLINE?

We want to share with you some basic guidelines for discipline to help you develop and implement your style. But before we discuss specific methods we need to understand what discipline is and what it is not.

Discipline Versus Punishment

There is a major difference between discipline and punishment. Punishment is past-oriented. Punishment is paying your child back for hurting you in some way. Punishment says, "You ruined my day, so I'm going to ruin yours." Its motive is revenge. We are clearly instructed not to take revenge (Romans 12:19). Only the Lord knows how much vengeance is dished out in the name of discipline.

A humbled mother told me about an incident of vengeance she had with her daughter. "Neil, Mandy destructively poked several small holes in my toothpaste tube, so I did the same to her tube of toothpaste. 'See how you like it,' I said to her. Then Mandy looked at me with a crushed expression on her face. 'You're not supposed to return evil for evil,' she said. I suddenly realized that my act of revenge benefited neither of us."

Discipline is future-oriented. In Hebrews we read: "All discipline for the moment seems not to be joyful, but sorrowful; yet to those who have been trained by it, afterwards it yields the peaceful fruit of righteousness" (12:11).

We don't punish our children for doing something; we discipline them so they won't do it again. Discipline superintends future choices. Discipline is proof of our love, not license to even the score.

Discipline Versus Judgment

Discipline is related to behavior while judgment is related to character. Suppose you catch your son telling a lie and confront him about it: "Son, what you just said isn't true." Are you judging him? Absolutely not. You made an observation about his wrong behavior and confronted him about it to change that behavior. But suppose you said, "Son, you're a liar." That's judgment. You're attacking his character.

Discipline is not character-assassination. When you attack your child's character you can expect him to be defensive. And if you try to overpower his defensiveness with words like "stupid kid," "dummy," "clumsy," or "lazy slob," you may crush his spirit.

If we could memorize and obey just one Bible verse, half of our family problems would disappear overnight: "Let no unwholesome word proceed from your mouth, but only such a word as is good for edification according to the need of the moment, that it may give grace to those who hear" (Ephesians 4:29). Verse 30 reminds us that God is grieved to see His children put each other down verbally. We are to be a building crew not a wrecking crew, especially with our children.

Furthermore, when you attack your child's character there is nothing he can do about it. He may want to become a better person, but he can't change his character on the spot, especially when you are attacking it. But when you confront him about his behavior he can do something about it immediately. He can confess it, ask forgiveness for it, and choose to change. And he doesn't feel rejected or wounded in the process.

Rules to Live By

All discipline must be based on prior instruction. It isn't right to discipline your child for doing something he wasn't told was wrong. Therefore, rules must be established and communicated. In order for rules to be effective they must be defensible, definable, and enforceable. Let's consider each of these separately.

Rules must be defensible. There are two issues at stake in defending your rules. The first is obedience. If you are simply giving an order like mow the lawn, and your child challenges you by asking why, you have every right to answer, "Because I told you to do it." Your command has nothing to do with rules, but it has everything to do with obedience. The child is questioning whether you have the right to give the order and testing to see if he really has to obey it. As long as your directive is legitimate you had better win these contests of the will. When your child questions your authority to direct his behavior, answer him decisively with actions as well as words while remaining in complete control of yourself.

One of the great lessons I learned early on the farm was to obey. If my dad told me to run to the shop and get a wrench, he meant run. If I walked instead of ran I soon learned that I'd have been better off to keep walking! I learned early to take orders and not to question my father's directives.

The second issue in defending rules is the legitimacy of the rules themselves. Do you have a balanced biblical basis for your rule? Are you aware of the practical issues involved in enforcing the rule? For example, before you make a rule, "No secular music in our home; only Christian music is allowed," you need to determine if it's a legitimate rule. Ask yourself several questions: Do we allow secular music when it comes into our home through the TV instead of the stereo? If so, how will I explain the difference to my child? Do I listen to secular music myself? Are all kinds of secular music and entertainment bad? Are all kinds of Christian music good? Is it realistic to ask my child not to listen to the same music his friends listen to?

Rules should make sense to a child. If they don't his approach to authority will be based on law instead of grace (2 Corinthians 3:6). External obedience alone is not enough; internal conviction is the ultimate goal. Kids need to know that rules are not for the good of the parents but for the good of the child. That's how they learn that God's rules are protective, not restrictive. You're not out to keep your child from having fun, nor is God. You are striving to help your child grow up within God's moral boundaries. Only there will he be protected from the evil one and live a healthy, productive life in peace and freedom. The best defense your child has against Satan is a righteous life. Your carefully planned rules will help guide him into that righteous life.

A common mistake parents make is laying down a law that goes beyond what God would require. For example, the Bible teaches, "Do not be bound together with unbelievers" (2 Corinthians 6:14). Some parents use this verse to forbid their children from dating non-Christians, having them for friends, or even associating with them. That may be good advice in some cases, but don't make it a rule. There's a big difference between associating with non-Christians and being "bound together" with them.

Through the process of implementing defensible rules you will help your children develop sensible moral convictions and valid criteria that will sustain them during any crisis. They will learn to ask questions like:

Can I do this and still be a positive witness for Christ?

Can I do this and still glorify God in my body?

Would I want someone to treat my sister, brother, or me the way I am treating this person?

Will I violate the fruit of the Spirit by doing this?

If Jesus was with me now, what would I do? What would He do in this situation?

Rules must be definable. A rule prohibiting heavy metal music in the house is not a very good rule unless you define exactly what heavy metal music is. What you think is heavy metal and what your child thinks is heavy metal may be two different things.

In defining the more difficult rules, discuss them with your child before you put them into effect. This is important for two reasons. First, your child needs to know exactly what you mean. Second, after discussing what is right, wrong, and reasonable with him, you may want to adjust the rules. When you take your child into consideration this way you convey respect, establish good communication, and create a climate of acceptability. You show that you care more about your child than about the rules. Remember: Rules without relationship lead to rebellion.

Rules must be enforceable. If you don't follow through with your rules you are baiting your children to disobey them. Consistency is the most difficult task in discipline.

Children can wear you down. It is better to be consistent with a few rules than inconsistent with many.

I worked my way through engineering school as a dorm master and wrestling coach at a private school. One evening I was called in to monitor 150 junior and senior high students during 90 minutes of evening study hall. The kids didn't want to be there, and usually there were two adults to keep them quiet and in the books. But this time I was alone.

Being the wrestling coach helped, but I realized that I was going to have trouble enforcing discipline all by myself. So as soon as the period began I announced that the first student caught talking would have to come up front and stand on my desk until he caught another person talking, then that person would take his place. They watched each other like hawks! In 90 minutes only three kids had to stand on the desk. In the meantime I sat in the corner doing my own homework. Half of discipline is just being more clever than your kids!

SETTING YOUR CHILD FREE

Every normal child wants to be free, and every normal parent wants his child to be free eventually. A young teenager's idea of freedom is having the right to do his own thing. That isn't freedom; that's license. The kind of freedom we have in Christ is the freedom to live responsible lives. If we learn to make right choices we will be free from our past, free from the powers of darkness, and free from the slavery of sin (2 Corinthians 3:17). Guiding your child to live a responsible, liberated life in Christ is a major responsibility in your parenting.

When our daughter Heidi was nearing her twelfth birthday, I took her out to lunch for a special talk about freedom. I read to her Luke 2:52: "Jesus kept increasing in wisdom and stature, and in favor with God and men." Then I drew a simple diagram on a slip of paper (see Figure 10a) and shared the following thoughts.

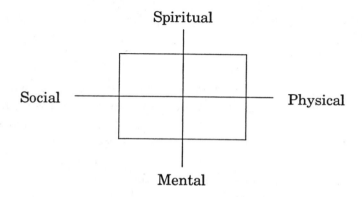

Figure 10a: Four areas of growth.

"Honey, Jesus wants you to be like Him and grow spiritually, physically, socially, and mentally. Right now you feel a little boxed in as my picture shows. I'm sure you want the freedom to be what God wants you to be, and your mother and I want that for you, too.

"Look at these four areas of growth. Spiritually, God wants you to have a great relationship with Him and grow to be like Him. To do that you have to know the Word of God. You also need to learn how to pray and walk by faith in the power of the Holy Spirit. You have to work at your relationship with God just like any other relationship. Your mom and I tuck you into bed each night and pray with you. We take you to Sunday school, pay your way to Christian camps, and encourage you to read your Bible. But someday, Honey, we won't be here to do that for you. You will go off to college or get a job, and you will hopefully do those things on your own.

"Physically, we help you wash your clothes and tell you to take a bath, brush your teeth, and eat the right foods. We buy all your clothes, and we encourage you to exercise and take care of your body. We hope you will develop some good habits and do even better when you're on your own.

"Socially, we take you places and encourage you to have your friends over to our house. We have tried to teach you how to get along with people and resolve conflicts when they arise. At times we have stepped in between you and your brother when you weren't getting along. But someday we won't be here to do that. It is our prayer that you will know how to get along with people and choose friends who will help you in your walk with God.

"Mentally, you are doing well in school. We still have to tell you to do your homework and turn it in on time. But if you go to college, you will have to survive on your own study habits. We won't be there to tell you when to go to sleep and when to do your homework. You will be on your own.

"You see, Honey, the outer lines on this square show where you are right now. They are the boundaries we have set for you to live within. But we want to keep expanding those boundaries so that every year you will have more freedom to make your own choices. We will give you more freedom each year if you will become more responsible each year. For example, we still have to tell you to clean your room. But if you will assume responsibility for your room, we will let you do what you want to do with your room.

"In a few years you can start dating when you show that you are ready. The first year you will only be able to stay out until about 10:00 P.M., depending on where you go. If you do well with that rule, we will expand the time. That will be true for every area of your life. When you show that you are responsible and can be trusted, we will give you more freedom. That's the way Jesus deals with all of us. In a parable He said: "Well done, good and faithful servant! You have been faithful with a few things; I will put you in charge of many things" (Matthew 25:21 NIV).

"Your mother and I will not decide how much freedom you have; you will decide that by how responsibly you live. We want to work with you to secure your freedom as you show yourself responsible. When you are 18, hopefully there will no longer be a box around you. You will be on your own and free do whatever God wants you to do."

Parenting is an 18-year process of letting go. God designed husband and wife to cling together, but He designed children to eventually leave their parents (Matthew 19:5). At that point your child's primary identity changes from being your child to being God's child. He is no longer dependent on you but on God. And his protection is no longer your responsibility but God's. If you discipline your child correctly now, hopefully he will make right decisions as an adult.

DIFFERENT METHODS FOR DIFFERENT KIDS

Disciplining each of your children the same way is not what makes you a fair parent. Holding the same standards and values for each child is what makes you fair. Your discipline methods may differ from child to child because each child is different. Spanking may be effective for one but totally ineffective for another. You need to discover and employ the methods that are effective for each individual child. Here are six methods to consider.

1. Communication

Any discipline method should start with communication. Make a clear statement of your expectations for a given situation and the consequences for disobedience. Ask your child to repeat what you say to make sure he understands. Then invite his questions and comments.

Some parents don't realize that a verbal confrontation after disobedience is a powerful means of discipline. Many kids would rather face a paddle than receive a lecture. Even parental silence communicates volumes. For a child, sitting emotionally exposed before an authority figure is much more painful and shameful than a simple spanking.

What is the motivating deterrent behind a verbal confrontation? The fear of being called into accountability. We find that in our relationship with the Lord. We fear Him because we are going to stand before Him someday and give an account of our lives (2 Corinthians 5:10,11)—not to be punished but to be rewarded. Knowing that we are going to be personally accountable before the Lord is a great driving force in our lives. We want to hear Him say, "Well done, good and faithful servant."

Your child feels the same way about having to answer to you. He doesn't want to look bad in your eyes. That's why it's often difficult for him to confess his misdeeds in a confrontation. When you sit down with him it will be easy for him to say "I'm sorry," a little harder for him to say "Will you forgive me?" and hardest for him to say "I did it."

Helping your child learn to speak the truth in love will take a lot of love and skill on your part, especially if your child is prone to lying. If you allow him to establish a pattern of deception as a means of avoiding confrontation, you are in for a lot of pain during his adolescence. You must work toward honest confession every time or the confrontation method will be ineffective.

The shame of accountability your child experiences during a verbal confrontation will be an effective deterrent to future disobedience. Don't ruin the impact by adding uncontrolled anger. It is harder for your child to look into the eyes of love when he is guilty than to look into the eyes of vengeance. The latter will frighten him but not necessarily shape his will for the future. The former will build in him an inner conviction that will stand him in good stead when he is tempted again to the same act of disobedience.

2. Natural Consequences

Some children are effectively disciplined when they must experience the natural consequences of their disobedience. For example, if your child fools around and misses his bus at school, you may choose to let him walk home instead of picking him up yourself. If he procrastinates on a school project you have urged him to complete, let him receive a bad grade instead of bailing him out by doing the project yourself. For many children the pain of the natural consequence is enough to prompt a change in behavior the next time. Strong-willed children may respond best to this means of discipline. They often have to learn the hard way.

Use wisdom when employing this method. Some natural consequences may be too severe when other methods of discipline could be used. For example, making a child walk home from school alone may not be advisable in dangerous neighborhoods or bad weather.

3. Logical Consequences

Plan a negative consequence that is logically related to your child's misbehavior. Logical consequences are effective because they teach kids to be responsible. For example, if your child carelessly spills his milk, a natural consequence is for him to clean up the mess. When he's playing outside and waits too long before coming in to use the bathroom, you may assign him to wash, dry, fold, and put away a load of his own dirty clothes.

Logical consequences help avoid power struggles between the child and parent. They can also greatly reduce nagging, corrections, and spankings. When your child completes the consequence, the incident is over, and hopefully he has learned to avoid the problem in the future.

Using natural consequences for discipline will require some extra work on your part. For example, you may need to teach your child how to use a sponge mop, operate the washing machine, etc.

4. Reinforcement

Reinforcement is the activity of catching your children doing something right and rewarding their good behavior. Too often the only time our children get our attention is when they do something wrong. When you consistently reward good behavior, your child is more likely to repeat it.

The most common reward for good behavior is spoken praise: "Good job"; "I appreciate your helpfulness"; "I'm so happy that you cleaned up your own mess without being told." Every child needs this kind of affirmation, but the child who is starved for attention needs it most. Aberrant behavior is often a cry for attention. The reward can also be material or monetary, but the critical issue is the behavior being rewarded.

5. Extinction

For some children, negative behavior can be eliminated when the parent ignores it. If a child is having a temper tantrum, sometimes it's best just to let him have his tantrum and realize that it doesn't work. You are saying, "I'm not going to honor your bad behavior by paying attention to it." When your child cries because of pain, you'd better respond. You may have just pinned the diaper to his bottom! But if he cries just to get attention, sometimes the best thing to do is let him cry. If you respond to his every whimper, he may whimper all his life.

6. Spanking

Spanking is certainly biblical, but it's not necessarily the best means of discipline for all children. Spanking is a negative reinforcer. The child gets the message that misbehavior can be painful, and so he chooses to avoid the pain by eliminating the behavior. It's like using electric fencing to keep cattle within certain limits. They find that it's painful trying to escape the boundaries, but no permanent damage is done.

If you spank, avoid doing so with your hand as much as possible. Reserve your hands to be used as instruments of love. Use an instrument that will sting but not injure. Also, never spank your child in anger. Your goal is to apply physical pain with a loving attitude so that the negative behavior is not likely to be repeated.

No matter what discipline method you employ, make

sure that you administer it in love. Before, during, and after discipline, make sure you communicate your love to your child. He needs to know that you love him more than you dislike his negative behavior.

The greatest gift you can give your child is yourself. Your loving attention to him and his needs is the most effective shaping tool at your disposal. Spend time with each child. Put their special events on your calendar and consider them important appointments. Remember: You will stand before God some day and give an account of your stewardship with the life He has entrusted to you.

Also be aware that your years of disciplining your child are numbered, as these lines from an unknown author beautifully describe:

> One of these days you'll shout, "Why don't you kids grow up and act your age?" And they will. Or you'll say, "Kids, get outside and find yourselves something to do, and don't slam the door!" And they won't.
>
> You'll straighten the boy's bedroom neat and tidy—bumper stickers discarded, spread tucked and smooth, toys displayed on the shelves, hangers in the closet with clothes attached, animals caged—and you'll say out loud, "Now I want it to stay just like this!" And it will.
>
> You'll prepare a perfect dinner with a salad that hasn't been picked to death and cake with no finger traces in the icing, and you'll say, "Now there's a meal fit for company!" And you will eat alone.
>
> You'll say, "I want complete privacy while I'm on the phone. No dancing around. No pantomimes. No demolition crews. Silence. Do you hear me?" And you will have it.

No more plastic place mats stained with spaghetti. No more spreads to protect sofas from damp bottoms and dusty shoes. No more gates to stumble over in the doorway of the baby's room. No more Hot Wheels or Barbie dolls under the couch. No more playpens to arrange a room around.

No more anxious nights under vaporizer tents. No more cracker crumbs on the sheets. No more wall-to-wall water in the bathroom. No more iron-on patches. No wet, knotted shoelaces, pants with knees out, or rubber bands for pony tails.

Imagine a lipstick with a point on it, not having to get a baby-sitter for New Year's Eve, family washing only once a week, seeing a steak that isn't ground, marketing with only groceries in the basket. No more PTA meetings. No more car pools. No blaring radios or *Sesame Street* three times a day. No more washing hair at 9 o'clock at night. And no more wondering, "Where is the family car!" Imagine having your own roll of Scotch tape.

Think about it. No more Christmas presents made out of construction paper and will-hold glue. No more sloppy oatmeal kisses. No more tooth fairy. No more giggles in the dark. No knees to heal. No responsibility! Only a voice crying, "Why don't you grow up!" And the silence echoing, "I did!"

PART 3

xxxxxxxxxxxxxxxxxxxxxxxxxxxxxxxxxxxxxxxxxxxxxxxxxxxxxxxxxxxxxxxxxxxxxxxxxxxxxx

The Secure Child

xxxxxxxxxxxxxxxxxxxxxxxxxxxxxxxxxxxxxxxxxxxxxxxxxxxxxxxxxxxxxxxxxxxxxxxxxxxxxx

Chapter 11

PROTECTING YOUR CHILD FROM THE DARKNESS

xxxxxxxxxxxxxxxxxxxxxxxxxxxxxxxxxxxxxxxxxxxxxxxxxxxxxxxxxxxxxxxxxxxxxxxxxxxxxxxxxxxxxxxxx

S ean Sellers, the young man convicted of killing his parents while involved in Satan worship, made a startling statement about his participation in the occult. He claimed that if he had had a close family relationship, he might not have gotten into Satanism. Though far from being an authority on parenting or family matters, Sellers gives us something to think about as we consider how to protect our children from the influences of New Age, Satanism, and the occult. A primary means to guard your child from wandering into the darkness is to flood his life with the warmth and light of a Christ-centered family relationship. We would like to suggest seven specific ways you can do this in your home.

1. Lead Your Child to Christ

The first step in protecting your child from the influences of New Age, Satanism, and the occult is to help him establish a personal relationship with Jesus Christ. Don't assume that he's a Christian simply because you're a Christian and have taken him to Sunday school regularly. He must make a personal commitment of his life to Jesus

Christ as Savior and Lord, and who better to lead him to that commitment than his parent? Here are a few important guidelines for leading your child to Christ.

Pray for your child's salvation. You can't argue your child into becoming a Christian, but you can pray for him and allow God to prepare his heart to receive the gospel. Your child's salvation should be at the top of your prayer list. A sample prayer for a child's salvation is found in Chapter 12.

Tell stories. Kids often understand concepts better when they are presented through stories. Tell or read to your child Bible stories about people who were challenged to give their lives to Christ. For example, you might consider using: Jesus talks with Nicodemus (John 3); Jesus and the Samaritan woman (John 4); Philip and the Ethiopian (Acts 8); Paul and Silas with the Philippian jailer (Acts 16). Also, expose your child to good Christian children's books that present God's love and plan for salvation.

Give a simple gospel presentation. At some point you must clearly and lovingly share the gospel with your child and invite him to open his life to Jesus Christ. There are many excellent tracts available which summarize the gospel in terms a child can understand. Whether you use one of these tools or not, your presentation should include these basic truths:

God loves you and wants to give you peace, eternal life and abundant life (John 3:16; 10:10; Romans 5:1).

You are sinful and separated from God (Romans 3:23; 6:23).

Jesus paid the penalty for your sin when He died on the cross (John 14:6; Romans 5:8).

You must confess your sin and receive Jesus Christ as your Savior and Lord (John 1:12; 1 John 1:9; Revelation 3:20).

As you talk to your child about spiritual matters, be sure to speak at his level. Don't use Christian jargon or abstract theological terms ("saved," "repent," "justification," etc.) without thoroughly explaining their meaning in words your child can understand. Also, don't try to scare or manipulate your child into making a response. Simply present the gospel, answer his questions, and allow the Holy Spirit to bring him to the point of deciding to trust Christ.

Give a clear invitation. After you have explained the plan of salvation and are convinced that your child understands it, say something like, "Would you like to receive Jesus Christ right now?" If he responds negatively, accept his decision and continue to pray for him and share the gospel with him. If he says yes, lead him in a simple prayer by having him read it aloud or repeat it after you phrase by phrase. Here is a sample prayer you can use:

Dear Jesus, I know that I have sinned and need Your forgiveness. I now turn from my sins to follow You. I believe that You died on the cross for my sins and that You came back to life after three days. I invite You to come into my heart and life. I want You to be my Savior and Lord. Thank You for Your love and the gift of eternal life. In Your name I pray, Amen.

Review his decision. After leading your child in a prayer
of salvation, take a few minutes to talk through the following questions with him to help him understand what
happened to him:

> What did you just do? Why?
>
> What did Jesus do when you opened your heart to
> Him (see Revelation 3:20)?
>
> What did you become when you received Jesus into
> your heart (see John 1:12)?
>
> Where is Jesus right now?

Here's one final thought on this subject. It's possible
that you have been reading about leading your child to
Christ but have not personally received Christ. Jesus died
for children *and* adults. If you have never surrendered you
heart and life to Christ, why not take a few minutes right
now to pray the simple prayer suggested above? Committing your life to Christ is the most important thing you will
ever do. There's no greater joy than knowing God personally.

2. Put Christ at the Center of Your Home

Before the Russo family drives somewhere together, our
twin five-year-olds, Tony and Kati, always buckle the
middle seat belt between them in the back seat. That's
where Jesus sits. In a very simple way they are beginning
to understand that Jesus is always with us and involved in
every aspect of our daily life as a family.

A spiritually healthy family is one where Christ is at
the very center. Just as the planets revolve around the sun,

so a family should revolve around Christ. The most important part of this process is making sure that Christ is at the center of your personal life as a parent. As someone once said, "You can't share what you don't have." Like it or not, your child's initial perspective of the Christian life will come from the example of godliness you portray. Is Christ truly the center of your life? Have you allowed Him to invade every aspect of your work and leisure? Do your children see you depending on Him in every circumstance? Do they hear you talking about Him being with you, answering your prayers, protecting you, etc.?

Your words and example should clearly testify that Jesus Christ is the Lord of your life. You must acknowledge His presence, His uniqueness, His priority in your life, and His right to rule over you. You need to demonstrate seeking His will and endeavoring to walk in His ways. We're not saying that you must model perfection. You can't; you're not perfect. But you must model obedience and growth if you hope to develop a Christ-centered home.

With Christ at the center of your life you can help your child begin to focus his life on Christ. A spiritually healthy home has a God-consciousness about it—that is, every member is aware that Christ is present minute by minute and involved in what the family is doing. You can foster God-consciousness by praying and praising God together throughout the day, not just at mealtimes or bedtime. Talk with your child about the beauty of God's creation as you drive through the country. When you see people who are needy, talk about ways you can help them just as Jesus helped others. In these ways you will help your child see that loving Christ is more than just something you do on Sunday.

3. Establish Consistent Family Devotions

You can help insulate your child against dark influences by diligently nurturing him with Scripture and prayer. Colossians 3:16 instructs us: "Let the word of Christ dwell in you richly as you teach and admonish one another with all wisdom, and as you sing psalms, hymns and spiritual songs with gratitude in your hearts to God" (NIV). One of the best ways to teach and admonish your children consistently is by having a time of family devotions every day or as often as possible. Tony and Kati call our family Bible study time "commotions," and their description is sometimes appropriate as we try to impart spiritual truth to our five-year-olds!

Family devotions should be brief and simple, especially with young children. Read one or two Bible verses and discuss their application on your child's level. Or read from a Bible story book or a contemporary Christian storybook for children and discuss the scriptural principles involved. Other options for this devotional time may include reciting a Bible verse you are memorizing as a family or reviewing your child's Sunday school lesson. Conclude with conversational, down-to-earth prayer about the concerns of the family and each child.

Look for creative ways to impart biblical truths during devotions. For example, have each family member draw a picture of what was read or discussed, or act out a Bible story with each family member playing one of the characters. Or challenge an older child to summarize the verse or topic in his own words.

As these devotional times develop in your home, use the following questions to help you evaluate your child's spiritual growth. When you observe an area in need of attention, use your family devotions time to address it:

Is he learning to experience God's love and demonstrate his love for God?

Is he learning to talk about God at home and outside the home?

Is he learning to turn to Jesus with his fears, worries, and problems?

Is he learning to read the Bible, pray, and memorize verses?

Is he learning about sin and the consequences of his choices?

Is he learning to give a portion of his money to God?

4. Teach Biblical Values

With relative morality and values clarification permeating our society, it is important that you help your child understand and apply to his life biblical values. Moses instructed the parents of Israel: "These commandments that I give you today are to be upon your hearts. Impress them on your children. Talk about them when you sit at home and when you walk along the road, when you lie down and when you get up" (Deuteronomy 6:6,7). God is encouraging us in this passage to build biblical truth into everyday life and conversation. Kids need to know that God is interested and involved in every dimension of their lives and that the Bible applies to their daily lives. This is how we help them develop a biblically-based perspective on life.

A good place to start teaching biblical values is to encourage your child to ask "What would Jesus do?" in his relationships, his attitudes, and his behavior. If he asks

the question in a situation but can't explain what Jesus
would do, help him explore God's Word for direction. As he
searches the Bible with you for answers, he is forming a
solid biblical basis for his thoughts, words, and actions.
Fortifying his mind with God's truth is essential for resisting Satan's deception in New Age, satanic, and occultic
influences.

Before my most recent trip to the Soviet Union, my wife
(Tami) and I were talking with Tony and Kati about giving
to people who are less fortunate than we are. Specifically,
we talked about children in other countries who don't have
as many toys as our kids do. Tony and Kati decided that
Jesus would like them to share some of their toys with
needy children. So when I left for my trip I carried a small
bag of toys our twins had sent to share with the children in
the Soviet Union. Even at age five they are learning that
God's Word is the guide for their lives.

5. Celebrate Each Child's Uniqueness

Our society is into comparisons in a big way. So much
emphasis is placed on appearance and performance. Our
kids are growing up in a world that rewards the prettiest,
the fastest, the strongest, the wealthiest, and the smart-
est. As your child competes with his classmates, friends,
and siblings for recognition, Satan can take advantage
of his sense of inadequacy, disappointment, and failure,
tempting him to find acceptance and satisfaction by dabbling in the wrong thoughts and activities.

The healthy Christian home is one where differences in
appearance, ability, and performance are not allowed to be
a source of divisiveness. Each child must be accepted for
who he is and encouraged to celebrate his own uniqueness
as a child of God. This can be accomplished by affirming

and honoring each child regularly. For example, set aside one mealtime each week or month to honor a child. Prepare his favorite meal, and serve it on a "You're Special" plate. During the meal have other family members describe how they appreciate the honored guest. Keep these comments focused on character qualities rather than appearance or performance. Then do the same next week or next month for another child. (As your children grow older, they will probably want to include you in the rotation.)

Another way to celebrate the uniqueness of your kids is to show a genuine interest in their activities. For example, your Amy wants to play girls' softball while Lisa is interested in joining 4-H and raising animals. If you are more interested in sports than animals, you may be tempted to urge Lisa to switch to softball, or you may spend more time with Amy at the ballpark than with Lisa on the farm. But in order to affirm and encourage both girls, you need to invest your time in learning about and appreciating each one's special interest. Helping each child feel appreciated and special is crucial to building a spiritually healthy family.

6. Maintain an Environment of Love and Forgiveness

Everyone needs to know that he is accepted and loved, especially a child. The love you convey to your child must be unconditional in nature—love which continually says, "I love you no matter what you do." This is the nature of *agape* love: patient, kind, not envious or rude, not self-seeking, not easily angered, etc. (1 Corinthians 13:4-8). You must communicate that your love for your child is the same whether he brings home an *A* or an *F* grade, whether he hits a home run or strikes out. He needs to understand

that you love him just as much when you are disciplining
him for wrong behavior as when you are rewarding him for
right behavior.

For most of our kids, a significant expression of parental
love is the time we spend with them. One of the best ways
to build an environment of love and caring in your home is
to schedule quality *and* quantity time with your child.
Take walks together. Go to the park and play on the swings
or shoot baskets together. Or just sit down together for
friendly, one-on-one chats. It's not so much what you do or
even how much money you spend to do it that's important.
It's that you consistently reserve time to be together, talk
together, work together, and play together. Time together
communicates love.

Forgiveness is a significant element of unconditional
love. Kids need to be disciplined for their misbehaviors,
but they also need to know that you forgive them for their
offenses. Forgiveness is not always easy for us, but it is a
scriptural command (Colossians 3:13) that must be obeyed
in the home. Unforgiveness leads to bitterness which is
like cancer to the soul. Unforgiveness is one of Satan's
greatest avenues of opportunity in our lives.

When you discipline your child for misbehavior, it is
important to teach him to ask God's forgiveness and to
seek the forgiveness of any person he has wronged. For
example, if your child damages your neighbor's property
through careless play, you must help him own up to his
mistake, go to the neighbor to ask forgiveness, and offer to
make restitution for the damage done. When he offends
you or your spouse, he must be confronted and encouraged
to ask forgiveness. Once you forgive him, you must never
bring up the offense again in a critical manner.

Once again, the best way for your child to learn how to
confess his misdeeds and ask forgiveness is through your

example. It's humbling for me to ask Tony or Kati to forgive me after I've said or done something to hurt them. But when I do I am blessed to hear a little voice say, "Daddy, I forgive you, and I still love you." If you don't admit your faults and seek forgiveness from your children, you are not only opening yourself up to spiritual conflicts, but you are teaching your children to do the same.

7. Make Prayer a Priority

It's been said that Satan believes in prayer, not because he practices it but because he suffers from it. We need to help our kids recognize the invaluable resource for resisting the devil that is available to them in prayer. They need to learn that God is interested in everything that touches their lives—every circumstance, relationship, event, and problem—and that He hears and answers their prayers.

Prayer will become significant to your children as they see it practiced by you. How often do you pray together as a family apart from mealtimes and bedtime? Do you consistently bring the needs of your family before God in prayer? Do you turn to the Lord first or pray as a last resort? Do you pray consistently with and for each of your children? The importance you give to prayer in your home will significantly shape the importance your child gives to prayer.

Recently our family took a car trip of several hundred miles. As we drove along a rather remote stretch of highway, the car suddenly lost power, and we coasted to the side of the road. After exhausting my limited mechanical expertise, I realized that we needed help. I didn't feel right about leaving Tami and the twins alone while I went looking for a telephone, so we decided to stay together and hope a passing motorist would stop to help us. But the few cars that drove by just kept going.

After waiting for almost an hour with no help in sight, I finally turned to Tony and Kati and asked them to pray. They took turns: "Dear Jesus, please send someone to help make our car better." Their prayers were short, sweet, and to the point. And in less than five minutes they were answered when a highway patrolman drove up and help was secured.

Tony and Kati haven't forgotten that experience, nor have they forgotten that God hears and answers prayer. There's nothing like answered prayer in the family to motivate you and your children to pray.

One way to maintain that encouragement and motivation is to keep a family prayer diary. When you and your child pray about something, write down the date you prayed and the specific request of your prayer. Then when God answers the prayer, enter the date, and praise God together for his goodness, mercy, and faithfulness. Refer to the answers recorded in the prayer diary for encouragement when other requests are not answered as quickly. The prayer diary is something tangible in your home to remind your child that God hears and answers prayer.

In addition to praying *with* your child, you need to be praying *for* your child consistently and specifically. In Chapter 12 we discuss several ways you can guard your child from dark influences through prayer.

Chapter 12

PRAYING FOR YOUR CHILD

xxxxxxxxxxxxxxxxxxxxxxxxxxxxxxxxxxxxxxxxxxxxxxx

E sther was a godly mother of five children who had a militant unbeliever for a husband. The man took great delight in criticizing his wife. He made fun of her faith in front of the children and revealed her faults before their guests. He did everything he could to undermine her attempts to raise the children as Christians. Despite his opposition, all five of Esther's children grew up to be dedicated Christians.

Late in Esther's life, a friend who knew of her difficult home situation asked her how she managed to succeed in raising godly children under such circumstances. Esther replied, "I made it my goal never to criticize my husband and always pray with the children and read the Bible to them when I tucked them in at night." Here is a woman who accepted the challenge to be the wife and mother God wanted her to be. She had a goal that could not be blocked. She also knew that she must assume responsibility to do what she could and trust God for that which only He could do.

As we have seen in the previous chapters, there is much God has given us to do to guard and free our children from satanic seduction. But we can't do it all. Prayer is our primary means for declaring our dependence on God to do what we cannot do. In this chapter we will look at several practical ways to lift our children to God in prayer.

As you will see, most of the suggested prayers in this chapter are not simple little two- or three-liners. Don't try to dismiss your responsibility to pray for your child by zipping through a hasty prayer. The issue of your child's spiritual freedom and protection is too significant for that. Take time to pray specifically and thoroughly as these prayers suggest.

GIVING YOUR CHILD TO GOD

Paul wrote: "Let a man regard us in this manner, as servants of Christ, and stewards of the mysteries of God. In this case, moreover, it is required of stewards that one be found trustworthy" (1 Corinthians 4:1,2). A steward is a manager or superintendent of another's household. As Christians, we own nothing in the kingdom of God. Everything we possess belongs to God; we are to be trustworthy stewards of what He has given to us.

The most valuable possession God has entrusted to our care as parents is human life: our children. God allows us to enter into only one creative act, and that is procreation. We call them ours but, like everything else we possess, our children belong to God. We are merely stewards of the precious human lives God has allowed us to bring into the world.

A Prayer for a Child's Dedication

Baby dedication is a public declaration of parental stewardship. In this act we say, "This child belongs to God. We dedicate our child to God and commit ourselves to be faithful stewards of that which He has entrusted to us."

The account of Hannah is often read in conjunction with baby dedication (1 Samuel 1:1-28). For some reason God had closed Hannah's womb and she was childless. Greatly distressed, she prayed asking God to give her a son, vowing to give the boy to the Lord (verse 11). God answered Hannah's prayer, and she fulfilled her vow. After Samuel was weaned Hannah presented him to the Lord: "So I have dedicated him to the Lord; as long as he lives he is dedicated to the Lord" (verse 28).

Joseph and Mary also modeled the importance of giving our children to God: "When the days for their purification according to the law of Moses were completed, they brought Him up to Jerusalem to present Him to the Lord" (Luke 2:22). Like Joseph and Mary, we need to purify ourselves as trustworthy, obedient stewards and bring our children to the Lord.

Reformed churches and most liturgical churches combine the formal dedication of the child with infant baptism. Other churches who hold to believer's baptism by immersion see baby dedication as a separate act. Either way, the parents' act of presenting their children to God is based on a solid scriptural principle.

If you don't publicly present your children to the Lord as His steward, Satan may attempt to claim ownership. Since he is the god of this world, anything that is left unprotected, unclaimed, or unprovided for is fair game and potentially subject to him. Baby dedication/baptism is too often regarded as little more than an opportunity for the proud parents to show off their new child. Nothing of spiritual significance is expected to happen. But Satan has something spiritually significant in mind for your child, and it's not what you would want. Presenting your child to

God through public dedication is a primary way to protect him from Satan's destructive plans.

Consider using a prayer similar to the following to dedicate your child to the Lord:

> Dear Heavenly Father, I thank You for loving me and giving me eternal life in Christ Jesus. I am Your child, purchased by the blood of the Lord Jesus Christ, who gave His life for me. I renounce any claim of personal ownership over anything I have, and I announce my responsibility to be a good steward of that which you have entrusted to me. I dedicate myself to You as a living sacrifice, and I commit myself to know You and do Your will. I commit myself to bring up <u>your child</u> in the discipline and instruction of the Lord. I know that <u>your child</u> is a gift from You, and I dedicate him to You for as long as he shall live. I reject any claim that Satan may have on him; he belongs to the Lord Jesus Christ. I announce that Jesus paid the price for my child and that he belongs to Him. As for me and my house, we will serve the Lord. I do all this in the wonderful name of Christ Jesus my Lord. Amen.

A Prayer for a Child's Salvation

In no way are we more dependent on God as parental stewards than for the salvation of our children. We cannot cause them to be born again. But we can and must do all within our power to lead them to Christ by being the witnesses God wants us to be.

In addition, we must pray for their salvation. The apostle John wrote about the importance of prayer in bringing others to Christ:

This is the confidence which we have before Him, that, if we ask anything according to His will, He hears us. And if we know that He hears us in whatever we ask, we know that we have the requests which we have asked from Him. If anyone sees his brother committing a sin not leading to death, he shall ask and God will for him give life to those who commit sin not leading to death (1 John 5:14-16).

The context of these verses is the assurance of eternal life (verses 11-13) and assurance of answered prayer (5:14, 15). The word "life" in this passage is clearly spiritual life. A "brother committing a sin not leading to death" refers to a non-Christian who has not totally rejected the conviction of the Holy Spirit, which is the sin of unbelief or the "unpardonable sin." John is saying that God will give spiritual life to unbelievers in response to our prayers of faith.

This passage does not teach that we can choose the people we want to be saved, pray for them, and they will automatically be saved. But it does teach that prayer plays an integral part in the process of God bringing people to Himself. We know that the salvation of unbelievers is God's desire because He "desires all men to be saved and to come to the knowledge of the truth" (1 Timothy 2:4). God promises to respond to our prayers for the unbeliever in some fashion if the person has not hardened his heart.

Your child should be at the top of your prayer list. One of your primary roles as God's steward is to intercede for his salvation. Here is a prayer you can use for the salvation of your child:

Dear Heavenly Father, I bring your child before You. I stand against the blinding of Satan that would keep him from seeing the light of the gospel of the glory of Christ and believing (2 Corinthians 4:4). I take the authority that is mine because of my position in Christ, and I exercise that authority over Satan in regard to the child You have entrusted to me. In the name of Jesus, I take authority over speculations and every lofty thing raised up against the knowledge of God in the minds of my child (2 Corinthians 10:5). I stand against the strongholds in his mind that keep him from obeying Christ. By the authority that I have in Christ and in obedience to the Great Commission to make disciples, I ask You to free the mind of my child so that he may obey God. I declare myself and all that You have entrusted to me to be eternally signed over to the Lord Jesus Christ. Based on Your Word in 1 John 5:16, I ask You to give spiritual life to your child. I pray that You will enable me to be the parent You want me to be. May I never be a stumbling block to my child. Enable me to be a positive witness and a living epistle to him. I ask this in the name and authority of the Lord Jesus Christ. Amen.

COMMITTING YOUR CHILDREN TO GOD DAILY

Even as a faithful steward over your child you don't always know what he is thinking and you can't be with him everywhere he goes. You must depend on the Lord for your child's daily protection, direction, and growth. You may have dedicated him to the Lord and prayed with him to receive Christ as his Savior. But your ministry of prayer for him doesn't stop there. You are responsible to lift him to the Lord daily.

Job apparently understood the importance of daily prayer for his children, because he would "consecrate them, rising up early in the morning and offering burnt offerings according to the number of them all" (Job 1:5). When God pointed out to Satan Job's righteousness, Satan pointed to the hedge God had placed around Job, his family, and his possessions (verses 8-10), inferring that Job wouldn't be so righteous if God didn't protect him so well. Perhaps the reverse is true: The hedge of protection was the result of Job's godly life and his willingness to pray daily for his family. Of course, God then removed the protection and allowed Satan to do a number on Job and his family. Yet even without the hedge "Job did not sin nor did he blame God" (verse 22).

The story of Job gives us several important principles about parenting and prayer.

Satan is actively looking for ways to destroy your family: you and your children. And the more righteous you are, the more interested he is in attacking you.

You and your children are utterly dependent on God for your spiritual protection.

God will put a hedge of protection around your family in response to your godly living and dependent prayer.

But God may also remove your protection if it will serve a greater purpose.

Suffering is the result of sin. However, even the righteous may suffer for doing what is right, but never without a purpose (2 Timothy 3:12).

Should suffering come to your family, you must continue to trust the Lord, pray, and not try to justify yourself.

God will make everything right in the end for parents who trust and love Him.

A Prayer for Protection

How did you feel when your first child walked out of the house for his first day at school? If your children are still at home, how do you think you'll feel on that special day? You may lament, "There he goes, off into the hostile world without me!" You're excited about his potential and growing awareness but fearful about the godless world he is about to encounter. You know you can't keep him home forever, and yet you wish you could for his own protection.

Your child doesn't go anywhere alone. The God to whom you have presented him is omnipresent. He will never leave nor forsake your child. You can call on Him daily for your child's protection. Here's a prayer you can use to ask for God's hedge of protection around your child:

Dear Heavenly Father, I ask for Your divine protection for <u>your child</u> as he is absent from me. I pray that You will put a hedge of protection around him so that all harmful influences cannot affect him. I commit him to You for Your care, and I assume all my responsibilities for training him in the Lord. I also assume the responsibility for the attitudes and actions in him that are the result of my training. I ask for Your Holy Spirit to guard his heart and bring to his mind all that he has learned from your Word. I thank You that, when he is tempted, You will provide him with a way of escape, and he will not be tempted beyond his ability in You to endure (1 Corinthians 10:13). I ask that the way he lives may be a witness to Your presence in his life. May whatever he does be done to the glory of God. I ask this in the precious name of my Lord and Savior Jesus Christ. Amen.

Prayer for a Rebellious Child

Have you ever tried to reason with a rebellious child? You can't do it! In fact, we are told not to: "He who corrects a scoffer gets dishonor for himself, and he who reproves a wicked man gets insults for himself. Do not reprove a scoffer, lest he hate you" (Proverbs 9:7,8).

What can you do? First, you must maintain a standard of personal godliness in your home. You can't compromise your convictions and expect God to bless your efforts. Being out of the will of God yourself and expecting your child to get into the will of God won't work!

Second, rebellion is a spiritual problem that requires a spiritual solution (1 Samuel 15:23). Allowing a child who is out of fellowship with God to control your home is allowing someone other than the Spirit of God to control your home, and that's wrong. Spiritual problems like rebellion can only be resolved by exercising the fruit of the Spirit and going to the Lord in prayer. Consider using the following prayer for a rebellious child:

Dear Heavenly Father, I ask in the name of the Lord Jesus Christ and through His shed blood that You will rebuke Satan and prohibit him from having any harmful influence on <u>your child</u>. Forgive me for any negative influence I may have had on him that prompted him to choose to rebel against You. I pray that You will give me grace to ask his forgiveness for my negative influence. I ask for the wisdom and grace to be the kind of parent that You want me to be. I confess the sins of <u>your child</u> (list all known sins) and assume my responsibility in his actions. I pray that You will build a hedge of thorns around him so that all harmful influences will lose interest. I pray that he will come to his senses and return to righteous living and loving relationships. I pray for grace to welcome him home or guidance to find a place of refuge for his good. Teach me to love my child but hate his sin. I ask this in the precious name of Jesus. Amen.

A Prayer for Your Child's Future

You cannot determine your child's future; God is the author and finisher of life and faith. James wrote: "Come now, you who say, 'Today or tomorrow, we shall go to such and such a city, and spend a year there and engage in business and make a profit.' Yet you do not know what your life will be like tomorrow. You are just a vapor that appears for a little while and then vanishes away. Instead, you ought to say, 'If the Lord wills, we shall live and also do this or that'" (James 4:13-15).

This is not license to be irresponsible about your child's future. But you don't know what God has in store for him. You can't mold your child into what you want him to be; you can only help him become what God wants him to be. The following prayer is an example of how to pray for your child's future:

Dear Heavenly Father, I ask for divine guidance for <u>your child</u>. I trust that You have already gone before him and prepared a place for him. You have known my child from the foundation of the world. I commit him into Your hands and pray for wisdom as to how I should relate to him in the future. I release him from all my expectations and entrust him to be what You want him to be. I pray that You will give him wisdom in choosing a life partner, and I pray for his future spouse. Should You bless them with children, may I be the grandparent You want me to be. I pray as Jesus prayed that you keep my child from the evil one and sanctify him in Your Word, for Your Word is truth. I ask this in the name of my Lord and Savior Jesus Christ. Amen.

Prayer for an Adopted Child

Adopted children are extremely vulnerable to demonic influence. Most of them are up for adoption because their natural parents did not want them and were poor stewards for the time the children were in their home. Satan attempts to claim ownership of anyone not claimed for Jesus Christ and brought under His authority. Since these children are often spiritually and emotionally unclaimed, they come to their adopted parents with spiritual problems even as infants.

We have counseled many godly couples who have adopted children only to see them all but destroy their families. If you are thinking of adopting a child, we recommend that you work with an agency that locates adoptive parents before the child is born. This way you can be present at the time of birth. You should dedicate your adopted child to the Lord immediately to assume stewardship and negate demonic influence.

If you already have an adopted child, lead him through the steps to freedom as explained in Chapter 13. Then pray over him as follows:

> Dear Heavenly Father, I thank You for entrusting your child into my care. I declare your child to be under Your authority. I dedicate this child to You and ask for Your protection and guidance as I commit myself to do all I can to lead him to an understanding of Your saving grace. I stand against all the devices of Satan that would keep this child in bondage. I renounce the sins of this child's ancestors and all curses that have been passed on from generation to generation. I announce that Christ became a curse for this child when He was crucified on the cross. I renounce all satanic sacrifices that have been made on behalf of this child and any claim of ownership that Satan may have. I announce that only the Lord Jesus Christ has any claim of ownership on him. I pray for a hedge of protection around this child all the days of his life. I ask this in the strong name of Jesus, who reigns supreme as the sovereign Lord of the universe. Amen.

A Prayer for Bedtime

The following is an example of a prayer you can teach your child to pray at bedtime. You may lead him in saying the prayer line by line until he can say it on his own. This prayer is based on Psalm 91:

> Dear God, I thank You that You are my Heavenly Father. I thank You for being in my life, in my room, and everywhere I go. I know that You are always with

me and will never leave me. I commit myself to You
and ask for Your protection. I trust You. I know that if
I'm ever afraid I can always call on You to rescue me. I
ask You to protect my mind tonight as I am sleeping.
Please bless and protect my home and parents. I love
You. I pray this in the name of Jesus. Amen.

A Prayer for Resisting a Spiritual Attack

Every child needs to know how to stand when he senses
a presence in his room or has some direct confrontation
with evil. Satan is under no obligation to obey your child's
thoughts since he doesn't have perfect knowledge of his
mind. Your child must take a stand verbally or express his
faith in a positive way.

For the small child, communicate something like Brittany's parents did: "Honey, Jesus is in your life and He is
bigger than they are, so you can tell them to leave in Jesus'
name." If your child can't say anything because of fear, let
him know that he can always talk to God in his mind, and
God will help him say what he needs to say. Encourage him
to memorize this paraphrase of 1 John 5:18: "I am a child of
God, and the evil one cannot touch me." If nothing else, all
he really needs to say is "Jesus."

A Prayer for Daily Life

As you prepare to send your child out into the world each
day, consider using a prayer similar to the following. The
goal is to teach your child the basic concepts of the prayer
so he can learn to pray them for himself:

Dear Heavenly Father, You are my Lord. I know that You love me and will never leave me nor forsake me. You are the only true and living God. You are worthy of worship. You are kind and loving in all Your ways. I love You and I thank You that I am alive in Christ. I submit myself to You and ask You to fill me with Your Holy Spirit so I can live my life free from sin. I choose to believe the truth which You have given in the Bible, and I reject all the lies of Satan. I refuse to be discouraged because You are a God of all hope. I believe that You will meet my needs as I seek to obey You. I know I can do everything You want me to do, because Jesus is my strength. I submit to God and resist the devil. I stand against Satan and all his lies, and I command him and all his demons to leave me. I put on the armor of God by believing and speaking the truth. I believe that Jesus is my protection. He never sinned, and He took my sin on Himself. I commit myself to be a peacemaker and to take the truth of the Bible and use it against all of Satan's dirty tricks. I submit my body as a living sacrifice to God. I will keep studying the truth so I can prove that what God wants me to do is good and perfect for me. I do all this in the name of Jesus. Amen.

As you pray for your children daily and through the problems and crises of their lives, you may feel at times like you are standing alone against the world, the flesh, and the devil. But you're really not. When you pray for your kids you are in good company. God's Word tells us that the Lord Jesus Himself and His Holy Spirit are committed to intercede for your children and for you (Romans 8:27; Hebrews 7:25). You never pray alone.

There is another level of prayer that is vital to your child's spiritual freedom. It is the prayer he prays to renounce Satan's involvement in his life and announce his dependence on Christ. Chapter 13 will help you lead your child through these prayerful steps to freedom in Christ.

LEADING YOUR CHILD TO FREEDOM IN CHRIST

xxxxxxxxxxxxxxxxxxxxxxxxxxxxxxxxxxxxxxxxxxxxxxxxxxxxxxxxxxxxxxxxxxxxxxxxxxxxxxxxxxxxxxx

F‌ive-year-old Danny was sent to the office of his Christian school for hurting several other children. All week he had been aggressive toward others and restless in class. His teacher said, "I'm puzzled by his recent behavior. It isn't like Danny to act this way." Danny's mother, a teacher at the school, had been recently enlightened about the reality of the spiritual world. When she came to the office she asked Danny if he loved Jesus. He covered his ears and shouted, "I hate Jesus!" Then he grabbed his mother and laughed in a hideous voice.

Danny's mother made an appointment to bring Danny to Ellen, one of the trained volunteers of Freedom in Christ Ministries. When Ellen sat down with him, she asked, "Do you ever hear voices talking to you in your head?"

Danny looked relieved that somebody understood. "Yeah, the voices yell at me when I'm on the playground telling me to hurt other kids. They yell until I do what they say."

"Danny, I have good news for you," Ellen said. "You don't have to listen to those voices anymore." She led Danny through the steps to freedom described in this chapter, having him pray the prayers after her.

When they were done Ellen asked Danny how he felt. A big smile brightened his face, and with a sigh of relief he said, "Much better!" His teacher noticed a calmness the next day. There has been no repeat of his aggressive behavior in school.

In Part One we discussed how even good Christian kids like Danny can become the targets of Satan's seduction through the influences of New Age, Satanism, and the occult in our culture. In Part Two we explored the role parents play in opening or closing windows of opportunity for satanic seduction through their attitudes and parenting activities. And in Chapters 11 and 12 we outlined specific steps you can take with your children to minimize spiritual conflicts in their lives.

But what should you do when you suspect that your child is experiencing a spiritual problem? Perhaps he is uncharacteristically disobedient, moody, reclusive, or destructive. He may be experiencing terrifying nightmares or complaining of unrealistic fears. It's possible that the enemy has somehow gained a foothold in your child's life. What can you do now?

In this final chapter we will present specific steps you can take with your child to lead him to freedom in Christ. These steps to freedom in Christ are specially adapted for children through age 13 from my book, *The Bondage Breaker*. If your child is 14 or older, I suggest that you use the steps to freedom explained in *The Bondage Breaker*.

THE TRUTH WILL SET THEM FREE

Your child can find his freedom in Christ in a quiet, controlled manner we call a "truth encounter." In other procedures for dealing with spiritual problems, called "power encounters," an outside agent (pastor, counselor, parent, or friend) bypasses the victim and confronts the demon directly. Proponents of power encounters contend, "Cast out the demon and the person's problems are over." But a power encounter may be superficial and potentially damaging because the tendency is to blame Satan for the problem and rely on an "exorcist" to solve it instead of helping the child assume responsibility for his life.

Jesus said it is truth that sets us free (John 8:32). In a truth encounter the demon is bypassed and the person with the problem is dealt with directly. Skeptics are quick to point out that this is not the procedure Christ modeled in the gospels, nor is it the method most deliverance ministries use. This concern is understandable since the gospels and the book of Acts are the only historical accounts where any procedure is actually illustrated. And since the epistles don't seem to provide instruction for such a procedure, some have questioned whether the church should even be involved in helping people get free from demonic influences. Some will even go so far as to say that there are no spiritual problems, only psychological ones.

The procedure presented in this chapter comes almost exclusively from the New Testament epistles. Satan was not defeated prior to the cross, so deliverance required an outside agent with special authority such as an apostle (Luke 9:1). But after Satan's defeat at the cross, the responsibility of spiritual freedom shifted from the outside agent to the individual. Each of us, including your child, is responsible to walk in spiritual freedom. You can't put on the armor of God for your child, believe for him, resist the devil for him, confess sin for him, or forgive others for him. All you can do is pray for him and help him understand what he must do in order to live a responsible life, stand

against Satan, and experience the freedom that Christ
purchased for him on the cross.

Are You Ready to Help?

Second Timothy 2:24-26 reveals the process of a truth
encounter and the qualifications for those who would help
others find their freedom in Christ: "The Lord's bond-
servant must not be quarrelsome, but be kind to all, able to
teach, patient when wronged, with gentleness correcting
those who are in opposition, if perhaps God may grant
them repentance leading to the knowledge of the truth,
and they may come to their senses and escape from the
snare of the devil, having been held captive by him to do
his will."

As you can see, the presence of God and a knowledge of
the truth are the basic ingredients for setting your child
free from captivity. When God and His truth are present,
the captive will come to his senses and escape the snare of
the devil.

These verses also establish the credentials you must
have in order to help your child experience freedom. First,
you must be the Lord's bond-servant. You must be sure of
your own identity and freedom in Christ before trying to
help your child. You cannot impart what you do not possess. If you are not free yourself, you need to walk through
the steps to freedom in Christ before trying to help your
child do so.

Furthermore, your relationship with your child must be
on solid ground. Are you quarrelsome or kind with him?
Are you patient when he wrongs you? Do you correct him
with gentleness? You may need to begin the procedure by
asking your child to forgive you for the times you have been
harsh, unkind, or impatient in dealing with him.

Leading an Older Child to Freedom (Ages 9–13)

This first section is for helping children who can read the prayers and statements themselves—ages nine to 13. Later in this chapter you will learn how to help a child who is too young to read.

In order for your child to realize his freedom from demonic influence, he must know that *he* is not the problem. Rather, you must help him understand that he *has* a spiritual problem for which he must assume responsibility. You must encourage him to share with you any mental opposition he experiences to what you are attempting to do. For example, the enemy may try to interrupt the procedure by filling the child's mind with thoughts like, "You're no good," "This isn't going to work," or "God doesn't love you." Urge your child to tell you what he's hearing in his head, and remind him that he doesn't have to pay attention to it.

Your goal is to help him get rid of those voices. He may be reluctant to tell you about them because he's afraid that you won't believe him or because the voices are threatening to hurt him. Assure him that Satan's only power is in the lie. As soon as your child speaks what he is hearing the lie is exposed and the power is broken.

During this procedure it is what your child chooses to renounce, confess, forgive, etc. that sets him free, not what you do. You are only the facilitator in the process. Since Satan is under no obligation to obey our thoughts, your child must pray the prayers aloud and assume responsibility to resolve the issues that are standing between him and God. Before you begin leading your child through the seven steps, pray this prayer with authority:

Dear Heavenly Father, we acknowledge Your presence in this room and in our lives. You are everywhere, You are all-powerful, and You know all things. We need You, and we know that we can do nothing without You. We believe the Bible because it tells us what is really true. We refuse to believe the lies of Satan. We ask You to rebuke Satan and place a hedge of protection around this room so we can do Your will. As children of God we take authority over Satan and command Satan to release (child's name) in order that (child's name) can know and choose to do the will of God. In the name of Jesus, we command Satan and all His forces to be bound and silenced within (child's name) so they cannot inflict any pain or in any way prevent God's will from being accomplished in (child's name)'s life. We ask the Holy Spirit to fill us and direct us into all truth. In Jesus' name we pray. Amen.

Binding Satan does not ensure total release for the victim. If that were the case then the epistles would simply instruct us to bind Satan and cast him to some distant planet. The Lord will cast Satan into the abyss in the last days, but until then he still roars around. However, we have all the authority in Christ we need to live in righteousness and freedom and carry out the ministry that God has called us to.

Your child may experience demonic interference during the early stages of the steps to freedom. Watch him closely, especially his eyes, as you lead him through the steps. If he starts to drift away mentally, ask him what he is hearing or seeing inside. Be aware that he may experience a severe headache or nausea. Usually the mental and physical interference will stop when he talks about them. If not, pray again for Satan to release the child.

If your child experiences excessive interference, slow down so he will be able to stay with you. Take a break if necessary to have the child get up and walk around the room to help him focus his mind. If in the process of going through the steps he wants to leave or he suddenly bolts from the room, let him go. He will probably return within minutes. Don't try to restrain him physically. Our weapons of warfare are not of the flesh (2 Corinthians 10:3-5). Prayer is our weapon against such attacks. You have sufficient control by exercising your authority in Christ to help your child do what he must do to gain his freedom.

Even though he may struggle through these steps, your child will learn a valuable lesson in the process: that he can win a spiritual battle whenever he is under attack. If you try to "cast out" a demon for him, he will believe it is necessary to call you every time he is under attack in the future. He needs to learn how to resist Satan and call upon the Lord for himself.

Throughout the following steps your child will be asked to pray prayers of confession and renunciation. Make sure he understands the meaning of these two terms. To confess means to admit an activity openly and agree with God that it is wrong. To renounce is to turn away from the wrong activity and determine not to do it again. Have your child read the prayers and statements aloud directly from the book or from written copies you have made of each prayer.

Step 1: Confessing and Renouncing Spiritual Counterfeits

Have your child pray aloud:

Dear Heavenly Father, I ask You to help me remember anything that I have done or that someone has done to me that is spiritually wrong. I want to experience your freedom and do your will. I ask this in Jesus name. Amen.

Read over the following list with your child. Place a check beside any activity he has participated in either voluntarily or involuntarily.

_____ Astral projection   _____ Ouija board
_____ Bloody Mary   _____ Table lifting
_____ Using spells or curses   _____ Automatic writing
_____ Spirit guides   _____ Fortune telling
_____ Tarot cards   _____ Palm reading
_____ Hypnosis   _____ Seances
_____ Black or white magic   _____ Dungeons and Dragons
_____ Blood pacts   _____ Anti-Christian music
_____ Non-Christian religions _____
_____ Other experiences _____

Ask your child the following questions and note his responses:

1. Have you ever heard or seen a spiritual being in your room?

2. Have you had an imaginary friend that talks to you?

3. Do you hear voices talking to you in your head?

4. What other spiritual experiences have you had?

For each of the activities above that your child has participated in, have him pray a prayer of confession and renunciation aloud. For example, if he has been involved in playing Bloody Mary, his prayer would sound like this: "Dear Heavenly Father, I confess that I have played Bloody

Mary. I ask Your forgiveness, and I renounce having played Bloody Mary."

Dear Heavenly Father, I confess that I _____.
I ask Your forgiveness, and I renounce _____.

Special Renunciation of Satanic Ritual: For the first five years of her life, 11-year-old Sarah lived with her mother in a witches' coven. Both Sarah and her mother had given their lives to Christ several months earlier, but they were still being harassed by demonic powers. They experienced nightmares, dreams of snakes, banging noises, etc.

Sarah was asked to renounce all the practices of the coven she had been subjected to, including three spirit guides who had been with her since she was three years old. After she renounced them by name the voices stopped. When she was finished, Sarah was asked how she felt. She answered, "I feel like I'm sitting in the lap of God!"

If your child has ever been involuntarily subjected to satanic ritual in some way, he needs to renounce that participation. There are specific activities that satanists use in all their rituals. Have your child read aloud the following statements renouncing his forced or unforced participation in satanism and announcing his identification with Christ.

Kingdom of Darkness

I renounce ever signing my name over to Satan or having my name signed over to Satan.

I renounce any ceremony where I may have been wed to Satan.

Kingdom of Light

I announce that my name is now written in the Lamb's Book of Life.

I announce that I am the bride of Christ.

I renounce any and all covenants or agreements with Satan.	I announce that I have a new covenant with Christ.
I renounce any sacrifices that were made for me where Satan could claim ownership of me.	I announce that I belong to God because of the sacrifice of Jesus on the cross for me.
I renounce ever giving my blood in satanic ritual.	I trust only in the shed blood of Jesus for my salvation.
I renounce ever eating flesh or drinking blood in satanic worship.	By faith I eat only the flesh and drink only the blood of Jesus.
I renounce all guardians and surrogate parents who were assigned to me by satanists.	I announce that God is my Heavenly Father and the Holy Spirit is my guardian.
I renounce every sacrifice made on my behalf by satanists by which they may claim ownership of me.	I announce that Christ is my sacrifice and that I belong to Him since I have been purchased by the blood of the Lamb.
I renounce any ceremony in which I was assigned to be high priest or priestess for satanic service, and I renounce Satan's possession of me.	I announce that in Christ I am of a chosen race, a royal priesthood, a holy nation. I am a person for God's own possession. I belong to Him.

Step 2: Confessing and Renouncing the Lie

Have your child pray aloud the following prayer

Dear Heavenly Father, I know that you want the truth from me and that I must be honest with You. I have been fooled by Satan, the father of lies, and I have fooled myself. I thought I could hide from You, but You see everything and still love me. I pray in the name of the Lord Jesus Christ asking You to rebuke all of Satan's demons by Your power. I have asked Jesus into my life, and I am Your child. Therefore I command all evil spirits to leave me. I ask the Holy Spirit to lead me into all truth. I ask You to look right through me and know my heart. Show me if there is anything in me that I am trying to hide, because I want to be free. Amen.

Now have your child read aloud the following statement of faith in order to announce his commitment to God's truth:

1. I believe that there is only one true God who is the Father, the Son, and the Holy Spirit. I believe that He made all things and holds all things together.

2. I believe that Jesus Christ is the Son of God, and that He defeated Satan and all his demons.

3. I believe that God loves me so much that He gave His own Son to die on the cross for all my sins. Jesus delivered me from Satan because He loves me, not because of how good or bad I am.

4. I believe I am spiritually strong because Jesus is my strength. I have the authority to stand against Satan because I am God's child. In order to stay strong, I am going to obey God and believe His word. I put on the armor of God so I can stay strong in the Lord.

5. I believe that I cannot win spiritual battles without Jesus, so I choose to live for Him. I resist the devil and command him to leave me.

6. I believe that truth will set me free. If Satan tries to put bad thoughts into my mind, I will not pay attention to them. I will not listen to Satan's lies, and I will not do what he wants me to do. I choose to believe that the Bible is true. I choose to speak the truth in love.

7. I choose to use my body to do only good things. I will not let Satan into my life by using my body in the wrong way. I believe that what God wants me to do is the best thing for me, so I choose to do God's will.

8. I ask my Heavenly Father to fill me with His Holy Spirit, guide me into all truth, and make it possible for me to live a good Christian life. I love the Lord my God with all my heart, soul, and mind.

Special Renunciation of Eating Disorders: Children and adults with eating disorders such as anorexia and bulimia are driven by Satan's lies to defecate, vomit, or cut themselves. Many believe they are purging themselves of evil. Thoughts of suicide are common for these people.

The typical person with an eating disorder is a female who is physically attractive. From the time she was very young she received strokes for her physical appearance. She became so body-conscious that her mind was fertile ground for the enemy's lies. Satan convinced her that her worth was based on physical appearance. Instead of controlling her body, she is controlled by her body (1 Corinthians 9:27). To be free she needs to renounce her false identity, affirm her identity in Christ, and focus on character development instead of physical appearance.

By the time she came for counseling, Alyce had starved herself down to 78 pounds by taking 75 laxative tablets a day. Every attempt to control her behavior had only resulted in the problem getting worse. As with the majority of eating disorder victims, Alyce had no idea of the spiritual battle going on for her mind. She didn't understand her identity in Christ. Years of counseling and chronic hospitalization ended when she finally understood that her worth is based on her identity in Christ, not her physical appearance. After finding her freedom in Christ, Alyce said tearfully, "I can't believe that I listened to all those lies!"

If your child is suffering from an eating disorder, have her renounce her behavior aloud as follows:

Kingdom of Darkness	Kingdom of Light
I renounce vomiting to purge myself of evil and reject the lie that my self-worth is based on my physical appearance.	I announce that all food created by God is good and that nothing is to be rejected by those who know the truth.
I renounce taking laxatives and defecating to purge myself of evil.	I announce that it is not what enters my mouth that defiles me but what comes from the heart.
I renounce cutting myself to purge myself of evil.	I announce that only the blood of Jesus can cleanse me.

Step 3: Confessing and Renouncing Unforgiveness

A child who harbors attitudes of unforgiveness is a wide-open

target for demonic influence. Have your child read the
following prayer aloud:

> Dear Heavenly Father, I thank You for Your kind-
> ness, patience, and love toward me. I know that I have
> not been completely kind, patient, and loving toward
> others, especially those who have hurt me. I've had
> bad thoughts and feelings about them. I ask You to
> bring to my mind the people I need to forgive. I ask
> this in the wonderful name of Jesus, who will heal me
> from my hurts. Amen.

Have your child make a list of people who have hurt him
in some way. Assure him that forgiving these people is
God's way of healing him. You may say something like,
"Forgiving another person is like removing a fishhook he
has put in you. It's hard because you have to remember the
pain. But if you forgive him you are no longer hooked to
him. Forgiveness is believing that God will deal with the
other person in the right way and heal you from the pain
he caused you."

To forgive others from the heart, your child must admit
his hurt and hatred. Have him go through his list of names
using the sample prayer below. For example, he may pray:
"Dear Heavenly Father, I forgive Jason for hurting me by
calling me 'ugly.'" Encourage your child to stay with the
first person on his list until all the pain has surfaced and
been forgiven, then go on to the next person.

> Dear Heavenly Father, I forgive (name) for (specific
> hurts and offenses).

Step 4: Confessing and Renouncing Rebellion

Have your child pray the following prayer aloud:

Dear Heavenly Father, You have said in the Bible that rebellion is the same thing as witchcraft, and disobedience is like honoring other gods. I know that I have disobeyed and rebelled in my heart against You and others that You have put in authority over me. I ask for Your forgiveness for my rebellion. By the shed blood of the Lord Jesus Christ I resist all evil spirits who took advantage of my rebellion. Amen.

Step 5: Confessing and Renouncing Pride

Have your child pray the following prayer aloud:

Dear Heavenly Father, I confess that I have been thinking mainly of myself and not of others. I have believed that I am the only one who cares about me, so I have to take care of myself. I have turned away from You and not let You love me. I am tired of living for myself and by myself. I renounce my pride and ask You to fill me with Your Spirit so I can do Your will. I give my heart to You and stand against all the ways that Satan attacks me. I ask You to show me how to live for others. I now choose to make others more important than myself and to make You the most important of all. I ask this in the name of Jesus Christ. Amen.

Step 6: Confessing and Renouncing Other Known Sins

Have your child read the following prayer aloud:

Dear Heavenly Father, I agree with You that I have done some wrong things. I ask You to help me remember all the wrong things I have done. I now confess and renounce (known sins).

After he has confessed his sins to God, assure him on the basis of 1 John 1:9 that God has forgiven him. If he still feels guilty about sins he has confessed, it is Satan falsely accusing him (Revelation 12:10). Remind your child that the Holy Spirit will convict him of sins in the future, but only so he can confess, repent, and be forgiven (2 Corinthians 7:9,10). Have your child read aloud the following prayer of assurance:

Dear Heavenly Father, I thank You for forgiving me for all my sins. I now command Satan to leave me, and I choose to live the right kind of life so I can be free.

Step 7: Renouncing the Sins of Ancestors

Nancy and her husband asked me to spend a few hours with them during a camp at which I was the speaker. They were above-average in intelligence, Christian commitment, and personal responsibility. But Nancy lamented, "Neil, we just can't get it together in our marriage." They had submitted to counseling previously, but with no resolution.

When Nancy told me that her mother and grandmother were deeply involved in Christian Science, I knew I needed to take her through the steps to freedom alone. During our time together Nancy revealed that, when she was born and placed on her mother's breast, her mother exclaimed, "This is not my child!" Then as she was praying through this seventh step, Nancy gasped in surprise at an insight the Lord gave her. "Why, I've had a curse put on me," she said. After she had renounced the sins of her mother and grandmother her countenance was changed. And in the next few weeks, so was her marriage.

When God gave the Ten Commandments, He revealed that iniquity can be passed from one generation to the next (Exodus 20:5). Children are especially vulnerable to Satan's access through this avenue, especially little children who haven't had the opportunity to get into drugs, sexual immorality, etc. Have your child pray the following prayer aloud to renounce known or unknown ancestral sins:

Dear Heavenly Father, I come to You as Your child, bought by the blood of the Lord Jesus Christ. I have been set free from the power of darkness, and I am now in the Kingdom of Jesus. I am spiritually alive in Christ and united with Him in the spiritual world. Jesus has broken all ties with and workings of Satan that were passed on to me from my ancestors. I therefore renounce and reject all the sins of my ancestors. Because I am owned by Jesus, I reject any and all ways Satan may claim ownership of me. I announce to all the forces of evil that I am forever and completely committed and signed over to the Lord Jesus Christ. I now command every evil spirit that is familiar with my family and every enemy of the Lord Jesus Christ in or around me to leave me forever. I now ask You, Heavenly Father, to fill me with Your Holy Spirit. I present my body to You so people will know that You live in me. All this I do in the name of the Lord Jesus Christ. Amen.

LEADING A YOUNGER CHILD TO FREEDOM (BIRTH–8)

Donny was two and a half years old and very hyperactive. He seemed to leave destruction in his wake wherever he went. He couldn't sleep at night and screamed in fear whenever he was around anything that was Christian in nature. Donny's mother, sister, and brother had recently left witchcraft, trusted Christ, and taken the steps to freedom in Christ. But Donny's problems just seemed to get worse.

Donny's mother brought him in to see one of our counselors. The counselor prayed over Donny, renounced Donny's previous involuntary involvement in witchcraft, and took authority over all spirit guides assigned to him. After the meeting Donny slept for the better part of two days. Two weeks later he returned for a visit. He was calm, his destructive behavior had stopped, and he had developed a regular sleeping pattern.

Children like Donny can't read through the prayers of confession and renunciation themselves, so a parent, pastor, or counselor must help them. If the child is old enough to understand the basic concepts and recite the prayers after you, invite him to do so. But if, like Donny, he is too young to understand, you must take spiritual responsibility for him. Place your hands on him and pray as follows:

Dear Heavenly Father, I bring my child to you. I declare myself and my family to be under Your authority. I acknowledge my dependency on You, for apart from Christ I can do nothing. I ask for Your protection during this time of prayer. Since I am in Christ and seated with Him in the heavenlies, I take authority over all that You have entrusted to me. I declare my child to be eternally signed over to the Lord Jesus Christ. I renounce any and all claims Satan has on my child. I accept only the will of God for myself and my family. I now command Satan and all his demons to leave my child. I ask for a hedge of protection around my child and my home. I submit myself to You and ask You to fill me with Your Holy Spirit. I dedicate myself and my child as temples of the living God. I ask this in the precious name of Jesus, my Lord and Savior. Amen.

The best thing going for you in dealing with a young child is his simple faith in you and God. When you tell him that God loves him, he believes it. When you assure him that God is bigger and more powerful than the devil, he accepts it as truth. Children in the Lord have the same authority to resist the devil that adults do. They simply need to understand their authority and how to use it.

Three-year-old Brittany was waking up every night terrified and running into her parents' room. She complained that something was in her room. Brittany hadn't seen any bad movies or lived long enough to commit any major sins that might cause the problem. Her parents were at their wit's end.

While attending a conference on spiritual conflicts, they began to understand what was going on. One evening they sat down with their daughter and explained, "Brittany, you have Jesus in your heart, don't you?" Brittany nodded confidently. "Jesus is bigger than anything that comes into your room at night. And because Jesus is in your heart, you can tell those scary things to go away in Jesus' name and they will."

Brittany didn't come into their room that night, The next morning she proudly announced, "They came into my room last night, but I told them to get out in Jesus' name, and they left!"

Young children have active imaginations that can be fertile ground for the enemy. If you discover that your child has an imaginary friend who talks back to him, he may have tapped into something he needs to renounce. New Age proponents are actually promoting such thinking and advocating that children invite spirit guides into their lives.

Take seriously a child's comments about his fears. If he complains of horrible nightmares or about something frightening in his room, encourage him to talk about it without judging him. If you ignore or make light of his experiences, your child will conclude that you don't care or understand. In either case he may never talk about it again. That's the worst thing that can happen, because Satan's influence may continue unquestioned and unchecked in his life. Take responsibility for your young child by reminding him of his authority in Christ and by taking a stand against the enemy in prayer.

Our children are precious gifts from God. Let's do everything we can to protect them against the seductive schemes of the devil by being the parents God wants us to be, surrounding them with a Christ-centered home, and lifting them to God in prayer. But when Satan gains a foothold in their lives, let's be quick to resist him in Jesus' name, and he will flee.

Bo 21-11-96

Bo 04-11-07

APPENDICES

xxxxxxxxxxxxxxxxxxxxxxxxxxxxxxxxxxxxxxxxxxxxxxxxxxxxxxxxxxxxxxxxxxxxxxxxx

GLOSSARY OF
NEW AGE TERMS

Age of Aquarius. Astrologers believe that evolution goes through cycles directly corresponding to the signs of the zodiac, each lasting approximately 2000 years. Advocates of the New Age say we are now moving in the cycle associated with Aquarius. The Aquarian Age will supposedly be characterized by a heightened degree of spiritual or cosmic consciousness.

Akashic Records. Assumed vast reservoir of knowledge. Some New Agers believe that the events of all human lives have been recorded in the Universal Mind or Memory of Nature in a region of space known as the ether.

Alchemy. Often associated with medieval folklore, this is a chemical science and speculative philosophy designed to transform base metals into gold. It is figuratively used regarding the change of base human nature into the divine.

Altered States. States other than normal waking consciousness, such as daydreaming; sleep-dreaming; hypnotic trance; meditative, mystical, or drug-induced states; or unconscious states.

Ascended Master. A highly evolved individual no longer required to undergo lifetimes on the physical plane in order to achieve spiritual growth.

Aura. An apparent envelope or field of colored radiation said to surround the human body and other animate objects with the color or colors indicating different aspects of physical, psychological, and spiritual condition.

Biofeedback. A technique using instruments to self-monitor normally unconscious involuntary body processes, such as brain waves, heartbeat, and muscle tension. As this information is fed to the individual,

233

he can consciously and voluntarily control internal biological functions.

Channeling. A New Age form of mediumship or spiritism. The channeler yields control of his perceptual and cognitive capacities to a spiritual entity with the intent of receiving paranormal information.

Chakras. The seven energy points on the human body, according to New Agers and yogis. Raising the Kundalini through the chakras is the aim of yoga meditation. Enlightenment (Samadhi) is achieved when the Kundalini reaches the "crown chakra" at the top of the head.

Clairaudience. The ability to hear mentally without using the ears.

Clairvoyance. The ability to see mentally beyond ordinary time and space without using the eyes. Also called second sight.

Consciousness. Mental awareness of present knowing. New Agers usually refer to consciousness as the awareness of external objects or facts.

Consciousness Revolution. A New Age way of looking at and experiencing life. The primary focus of the new consciousness is oneness with God, all mankind, the earth, and the entire universe.

Cosmic Consciousness. A spiritual and mystical perception that all the universe is one. To attain cosmic consciousness is to see the universe as God and see God as the universe.

Crystals. New Age advocates believe that crystals contain incredible healing and energizing powers. Crystals are often touted as being able to restore the flow of energy in the human body.

Dharma. Law, truth, or teaching. Used to express the central teachings of the Hindu and Buddhist religions. Dharma implies that essential truth can be stated about the way things are, and that people should comply with that norm.

Divination. Methods of discovering the personal, human significance of present or future events. The means to obtain insights may include dreams, hunches, involuntary body actions, mediumistic possession, consulting the dead, observing the behavior of animals and birds, tossing coins, casting lots, and reading natural phenomena.

Esoteric. Used to describe knowledge that is possessed or understood by a select few.

ESP. Extra-sensory perception. The experience of or response to an external event, object, state, or influence without apparent contact through the known senses. ESP may occur without those involved being aware of it.

Gnosticism. The secret doctrines and practices of mysticism whereby a person may come to the enlightenment or realization that he is of the same essence as God or the Absolute. The Greek word *gnosis* means knowledge. At the heart of Gnostic thought is the idea that revelation of the hidden gnosis frees one from the fragmentary and illusory material world and teaches him about the origins of the spiritual world to which the Gnostic belongs by nature.

The Great Invocation. A New Age prayer that has been translated into over 80 languages. The purpose of this prayer is to invoke the presence of the cosmic Christ on earth, thus leading to the oneness and brotherhood of all mankind.

Harmonic Convergence. The assembly of New Age meditators at the same propitious astrological time in different locations to usher in peace on earth and a one-world government.

Hologram. A three-dimensional projection resulting from the interaction of laser beams. Scientists have discovered that the image of an entire hologram can be reproduced from any one of its many component parts. New Agers use the hologram to illustrate the oneness of all reality.

Higher Self. The most spiritual and knowing part of oneself, said to lie beyond ego, day-to-day personality, and personal consciousness. The higher self can be channeled for wisdom and guidance. Variations include the oversoul, the super-consciousness, the atman, the Christ (or Krishna or Buddha) consciousness, and the God within.

Humanism. The philosophy that upholds the primacy of human beings rather than God or any abstract metaphysical system. Humanism holds that man is the measure of all things.

Human Potential Movement. A movement with roots in humanistic philosophy that stresses man's essential goodness and unlimited potential.

Initiation. An occult term generally used in reference to the expansion or transformation of a person's consciousness. An initiate is one whose consciousness has been transformed to perceive inner realities. There are varying degrees of initiation, such as first degree, second degree, etc.

Inner Self. The inner divine nature possessed by human beings. All people are said to possess an inner self, though they may not be aware of it.

Interdependence/Interconnectedness. Used by New Agers to describe the oneness and essential unity of everything in the universe. All reality is viewed as interdependent and interconnected.

Karma. The debt accumulated against the soul as a result of good or bad actions committed during one's life (or lives). If one accumulates good karma, he supposedly will be reincarnated to a desirable state. If one accumulates bad karma, he will be reincarnated to a less desirable state.

Kirilian. A type of high-voltage photography using a pulsed, high-frequency electrical field and two electrodes between which are placed on the object to be photographed and an unexposed film plate. The image captured is purported to be an aura of energy emanating from plants, animals, and humans that changes in accordance with physiological or emotional shifts.

Magic Circle. A ring drawn by occultists to protect them from the spirits and demons they call up by incantations and rituals.

Mantra. A holy word, phrase, or verse in Hindu or Buddhist meditation techniques. A mantra is usually provided to an initiate by a guru who supposedly holds specific insights regarding the needs of his pupils. The vibrations of the mantra are said to lead the meditator into union with the divine source within.

Monism. Literally means one. In a spiritual framework it refers to the classical occult philosophy that all is one; all reality may be reduced to a single unifying principle partaking of the same essence and reality. Monism also relates to the belief that there is no ultimate distinction between the creator and the creation (pantheism).

Mysticism. The belief that God is totally different from anything the human mind can think and must be approached by a mind without content. Spiritual union or direct communion with ultimate reality can be obtained through subjective experience such as intuition or a unifying vision.

New Age Movement. The most common name for the growing penetration of Eastern and occultic mysticism into Western culture. The words New Age refer to the Aquarian Age which occultists believe is dawning, bringing with it an era of enlightenment and peace. Encompassed within the New Age movement are various cults which emphasize mystic experiences.

Nirvana. Literally a blowing out or cooling of the fires of existence. It is the main term in Buddhism for the final release from the cycle of birth and death into bliss.

Numerology. The analysis of hidden prophetic meanings of numbers.

Pantheism. The belief that God and the world are ultimately identical; all is God. Everything that exists constitutes a unity, and this all-inclusive unity is divine. God is equated with the forces and laws of the universe but is not a personal being.

Paradigm Shift. Refers to a shift in worldviews. The so-called new paradigm (new model or form) is pantheistic (all is God) and monistic (all is one).

Planetization. New Age advocates believe that the various threats facing the human race require a global solution called planetization. It refers to the unifying of the world into a corporate brotherhood.

Poltergeist. German word for a noisy, mischievous, destructive spirit (demon).

Psi. The twenty-third letter of the Greek alphabet. A general New Age term for ESP, psychokinesis, telepathy, clairvoyance, clairaudience, precognition, and other paranormal phenomena that are nonphysical in nature.

Psychic. A medium, "sensitive," or channeler. Also refers to paranormal events that can't be explained by established physical principles.

Psychic Birth. A quickening of spiritual or cosmic consciousness and power. This new consciousness recognizes oneness with God and the universe. Psychic birth is an occult counterpart to the Christian new birth.

Psychokinesis (PK). The power of the mind to influence matter or move objects (see also telekinesis).

Reincarnation. The belief that the soul moves from one bodily existence to another until, usually after many lives, it is released from historical existence and absorbed into the Absolute.

Right Brain Learning. The right hemisphere of the brain is believed to be the center of intuitive and creative thought (as opposed to the rational nature of the left hemisphere). New Agers have seized on this as a justification to bring right brain learning techniques into the classroom. These techniques include meditation, yoga, and guided imagery.

Seance. A gathering of people seeking communication with deceased loved ones or famous historical figures through a medium.

Self-realization. A synonym for God-realization. It refers to a personal recognition of one's divinity.

Shaman. A medicine man or witch doctor.

Spirit Guide. A spiritual entity who provides information or guidance often through a medium or channeler. The spirit provides guidance only after the channeler relinquishes his perceptual and cognitive capacities into its control.

Syncretism. The fusion of different forms of belief or practice; the claim that all religions are one and share the same core teachings.

Synergy. The quality of "whole making"; the New Age belief in the cooperation of natural systems to put things together in ever more meaningful patterns.

Third Eye. An imaginary eye in the forehead believed to be the center of psychic vision.

Tantra. A series of Hindu or Buddhist scriptures concerned with special yogic practices for swift attainment of enlightenment; also the practices, techniques, and traditions of these teachings.

Telekinesis. A form of psychokinesis (PK); the apparent movement of stationary objects without the use of known physical force.

Trance. An altered state of consciousness, induced or spontaneous, that gives access to many ordinarily inhibited capacities of the mind-body system. Trance states are generally self-induced.

Visualization. Also known as guided imagery; refers to mind over matter. Visualization is the attempt to bring about change in the material realm by the power of the mind.

Yoga. Literally, yoking or joining; any system or spiritual discipline by which the practitioner or yogi seeks to condition the self at all levels—physical, psychical, and spiritual. The goal of the Indian religious tradition is a state of well-being, the loss of self-identity, and absorption into the Absolute or Ultimate Being.

Yogi. A master of one or more methods of yoga who teaches it to others.

Zen. A type of Buddhist thought best known for its emphasis on breaking down the commitment and attachment to the logical and rational ordering of experience.

Zodiac. The imaginary belt in the heavens that encompasses the apparent paths of the principal planets except Pluto. Divided into 12 constellations or signs based on the assumed dates that the sun enters each of these "houses" or symbols, the zodiac is used for predictions in astrology.

GLOSSARY OF
SATANIC/OCCULTIC TERMS

Black Mass. Held in honor of the devil on the witches' Sabbath. The ritual reverses the Roman Catholic mass, desecrating the objects used in worship. Sometimes the participants drink the blood of an animal during the ceremony. Often a nude woman is stretched out on the altar, and the high priest concludes the ritual by having sex with her.

Book of Shadows. Also called a *grimoire*, this journal is kept either by individual witches or satanists or by a coven to record the activities of the group and the incantations used.

Chalice. A silver goblet used for blood communions.

Coven. A group of satanists who gather to perform rites. There are traditionally 13 members, but with self-styled groups the number varies. A coven is also called a clan.

Curse. Invocation of an oath associated with black magic or sorcery intended to harm or destroy property or opponents.

Druids. A branch of dangerous and powerful Celtic priests from pre-Christian Britain and Gaul who are still active today. They worship the sun and believe in the immortality of the soul and reincarnation. They are also skilled in medicine and astronomy.

Magick. Magic that employs ritual symbols and ceremony, including ceremonial costumes, dramatic invocations to gods, potent incense, and mystic sacraments.

Magic Circle. A circle inscribed on the floor of a temple for ceremonial purposes. Often nine feet in diameter, it is believed to hold magical powers within and protect those involved in the ceremony from evil.

Magister. The male leader of a coven.

Magus. A male witch.

Necromancy. A practice in which the spirits of the dead are summoned to provide omens for discovering secrets of past or future events.

Necrophilia. An act of sexual intercourse with a corpse.

Occult. From the Latin *occultus,* meaning "secret" or "hidden." The occult refers to secret or hidden knowledge available to initiates, to the supernatural, and sometimes to paranormal phenomena and parapsychology.

Ritual. A prescribed form of religious or magical ceremony.

Runes. A northern European alphabet used by occult groups in secret writing. There are several forms of runering.

Santeria. A mingling of African tribal religions and Catholicism established by African slaves brought to the Americas and the Caribbean.

So Mote It Be. Words spoken at the end of an occult ceremony. Similar to "amen" in traditional religious services.

Talisman. A power object, usually an amulet or trinket.

Voodoo. An ancient religion combining sorcery and Catholicism. Those involved are extremely superstitious and are heavily involved in fetishism.

Warlock. Often used for a male witch, but it actually designates a traitor.

Wicca. The pagan end of the witchcraft spectrum.

Witch. A male or female practitioner of any sort of witchcraft.

Witchcraft. A practice of occultic arts, from wiccan-nature worship to satanic worship.

NINE STATEMENTS OF SATANIC DOCTRINE

The statements below represent the basis for modern Satanism. These statements are found in the satanic bible written by Church of Satan founder, Anton LaVey, and published in 1969.

1. Satan represents indulgence instead of abstinence.

2. Satan represents vital existence instead of spiritual pipe dreams.

3. Satan represents undefiled wisdom instead of hypocritical self-deceit.

4. Satan represents kindness to those who deserve it instead of love wasted on ingrates.

5. Satan represents vengeance instead of turning the other cheek.

6. Satan represents responsibility to the responsible instead of concern for psychic vampires.

7. Satan represents man as just another animal, sometimes better, more often worse, than those that walk on all fours, who, because of his "divine spiritual and intellectual development," has become the most vicious animal of all.

8. Satan represents all of the so-called sins, as they all lead to physical, mental, or emotional gratification.

9. Satan has been the best friend the church has ever had, as he has kept it in business all these years.

NOTES

Chapter 1

1. C.S. Lewis, *Christian Reflections* (William B. Eerdman's Publishing Company, 1967), p. 33.
2. *Los Angeles Times*, June, 1989, part V, p. 1.

Chapter 3

1. Walter Martin, *The New Age Cult* (Bethany House Publishers, 1989), p. 7.
2. James Patterson and Peter Kim, *The Day America Told the Truth*, (Prentice Hall Press, 1991), p. 204.
3. Russell Chandler, *Understanding the New Age*, (Word Publishing, 1988), pp. 20-21.
4. Nina Easton, "Shirley MacLaine's Mysticism for the Masses," *Los Angeles Times Magazine*, (September 6, 1987), p. 8.
5. Chandler, *Understanding the New Age*, p. 23.
6. Howard E. Goldfluss, "Courtroom Psychics," *Omni*, (July, 1987), p. 12.
7. Martin, *The New Age Cult*, p. 21.
8. Maxine Negri, "Age-old Problems of the New Age Movement," *The Humanist* (March-April, 1988), pp. 23-24.
9. *Los Angeles Times* (July 19, 1987), part VI, p. 1.
10. Chandler, *Understanding the New Age*, pp. 17-18.
11. *Time* (December 7, 1987), p. 62.
12. Martin, *The New Age Cult*, p. 15.
13. Jeremy P. Tarcher, "New Age as Perennial Philosophy," *Los Angeles Times* Book Review (February 7, 1988), p. 15.
14. Patterson and Kim, *The Day America Told the Truth*, p. 201.
15. Ibid, pp. 25, 27.
16. *Time* (December 7, 1987), p. 72.

Chapter 4

1. "A Generation that Failed," Presidential Youth Issues Forum, UCLA, (June, 1988).

2. Johanna Michaelsen, *Like Lambs to the Slaughter* (Harvest House Publishers, 1989), p. 43.
3. Daniel Druckman and John A. Swets, *Enhancing Human Performance* (National Academy Press, Washington, DC., 1988), p. 3.
4. Martin, *The New Age Cult*, p. 63.
5. Jack Canfield, "The Inner Classroom: Teaching with Guided Imagery" (1981).
6. Lori Ann Pardau and Timothy A. Bittle, "What is Johnny Being Taught?" *Citizen Magazine* (Focus on the Family, January, 1990), p. 4.
7. Barbara Clark, *Growing up Gifted: Developing the Potential of Children at Home and at School* (Merrill Publishing Co., 1983), pp. 592-93.
8. Mel and Norma Gabler, *What Are They Teaching Our Children?* (Victor Books, 1985), p. 22.
9. Paul Vitz, *Censorship: Evidence of Bias in Our Children's Textbooks* (Servant, 1986), p. 1.
10. Deborah Mendenhall, "Nightmarish Textbooks Await Your Kids," *Citizen Magazine* (Focus on the Family, September 17, 1990), pp. 2-3.
11. Pardou and Bittle, "What Is Johnny Being Taught?" p. 4.
12. Bob Simonds, National Association of Christian Educators, *Citizens for Excellence Newsletter*, (May 1990), pp. 2-5.
13. William G. Sidebottom and Frank York, "They Teach New Age in New Mexico's Schools," *Citizen Magazine* (July 1985), p.10.

Chapter 5

1. *Citizen Magazine*, (Focus on the Family, October 1989), p. 6.
2. *People*, (December 1, 1986), p. 157.
3. Geoffrey Smith, "Dungeons and Dollars," *Forbes Magazine* (September 15, 1980), p. 139.
4. Greg Johnson, "Breaking out of Satanism," *Breakaway* (May, 1990), p. 18.
5. Edmond Gruss, *The Ouija Board* (Moody Press, 1986), pp. 7-8.
6. *USA Today* (November 30, 1988), p. 3A.
7. Bob Larson, *Satanism* (Thomas Nelson Publishers, 1989) p. 66.
8. Stephen Arterburn and Jim Burns, *Drug-proof Your Kids* (Focus on the Family Publishing, 1989), p. 23.
9. "Alcohol Use and Abuse in America," *The Gallup Report*, (No. 265, October, 1987), p. 3.
10. *Los Angeles Times* (October 19, 1988), p. 21.
11. *Rising to the Challenge* video, Parents' Music Resource Center.

12. James Dobson and Gary Bauer, *Children at Risk* (Word Publishing, 1990), p. 65.
13. Michaelsen, *Like Lambs to the Slaughter*, p. 267.
14. Tamara Jones, "Experts Debate Influence of Violent Music on Youths," *Los Angeles Times* (October 19, 1988), p. 24.
15. Patrick Goldstein, "It's Not Easy Being Notorious," *Los Angeles Times* (May 5, 1991), p. 31.

Chapter 8
1. D.L. Thomas and A.J. Weigert, "Socialization and Adolescent Conformity to Significant Others: A Cross-National Analysis," *American Sociological Review*, vol. 36 (October, 1971), adapted from pp. 835-47.

Chapter 9
1. Lawrence O. Richards, *Youth Ministry* (Zondervan, 1972), pp. 139-45.

xx

The content of this book has been professionally
videotaped. These tapes are available for churches
and other groups or individuals. For information
concerning this and other resources and a schedule
of Neil Anderson's conference ministry, write to:

Freedom in Christ Ministries
491 E. Lambert Road
La Habra, CA 90631

Steve Russo is preparing a four-part video series
for teenagers. For information about this and other
resources and a schedule of Steve Russo's speaking
and campaign ministry, write to:

Steve Russo Evangelistic Team
P.O. Box 1549
Ontario, California 91762

xxxxxxxxxxxxxxxxxxxxxxxxxxxxxxxxxxxxxxxxxxxxxxxxxxxxxxxxxxxxxxxxxxxxxxxxxxxxxxxx

• • • • • • • • • • • •

The Seduction
of Our Children

*Audio & Video Tape Series
by Dr. Neil Anderson*
(includes syllabus)

Featuring topics from real life:

- God's Answer
- Identity & Self-Worth
- Discipline

- Styles of Communication
- Spiritual Conflict and Prayer
- Steps to Freedom

*A resource to help today's parents
deal with today's problems*

AVAILABLE FROM

Freedom in Christ Ministries
491 E. Lambert Road
La Habra, California 90631
(213) 691-9128

Write of call for order form of available materials on spiritual
conflicts and biblical counseling.
Visa and MasterCard accepted by phone.

• • • • • • • • • • • •

More Resources from Neil Anderson and Freedom in Christ to help you and those you love find freedom in Christ

Books

Victory Over the Darkness
The Bondage Breaker
Helping Others Find Freedom
  in Christ
Released from Bondage
Walking in the Light
A Way of Escape
Setting your Church Free
Living Free in Christ
Daily in Christ
The Seduction of Our
  Children
Spiritual Warfare
Stomping Out the Darkness
  (Youth)
The Bondage Breaker Youth
  Edition
To My Dear Slimeball

Personal Study Guides

Victory Over the Darkness
  Study Guide
The Bondage Breaker
  Study Guide
Stomping Out the Darkness
  Study Guide
The Bondage Breaker
  Youth Edition Study Guide

Teaching Study Guides

Breaking Through to Spiritual
  Maturity (Group Study)
Helping Others Find Freedom
  In Christ (Study Guide)
Busting Free
  (Youth Study Guide)

Other Good
Harvest House Reading

THE DEVIL'S PLAYGROUND
by *Steve Russo*

What teens face today is challenging and frightening. Popular youth speaker Steve Russo gives young people resources and guidance to stand up to Satan's attacks with a battle plan based on who they are in Christ.

LIKE LAMBS TO THE SLAUGHTER—
Your Child and the Occult
by *Johanna Michaelsen*

Dungeons and Dragons, Saturday morning cartoons, Star Wars, E.T., yoga, spirit guides, guided imagery and visualization, storybooks on the occult—are these calculated efforts to turn our children into a generation of psychics, shamans, and channelers? Michaelson scrutinizes the New Age Movement as it relates to children.

SUCCESSFUL SINGLE PARENTING
by *Gary Richmond*

Author Gary Richmond offers practical help and suggestions to single parents in this valuable guide to successful single parenting. *Successful Single Parenting* provides answers to the toughest questions single parents face. Here is a resource of information and encouragement that parents can turn to again and again.

PURITY UNDER PRESSURE
by *Neil Anderson* and *Dave Park*

In a reassuring style, popular spiritual conflicts counselor Neil Anderson and Freedom in Christ youth director Dave Park helps teens grasp the spiritual truths behind the pressures and temptations they face. *Purity Under Pressure* provides powerful tools and step-by-step instructions on breaking free from sin patterns and building godly relationships. Ideally suited for youth groups or individual study.

THE BONDAGE BREAKER
by *Neil Anderson*

Jesus intends for us to win the spiritual battles that confront us daily, and He has provided everything we need to gain the victory. Yet instead of experiencing victory, we often find ourselves trapped in defeat—overcome with frustration, bitterness, and discouragement. If you have ever found yourself enslaved by negative thought patterns, controlled by irrational feelings, or caught in habitual sinful behavior, Neil Anderson can help you understand the strategy of Satan and fight back.

THE BONDAGE BREAKER YOUTH EDITION
by *Neil Anderson* and *Dave Park*

The bestselling *Bondage Breaker* rewritten for youth who face peer pressure, sexual temptation, insecurity, and fear. Offers practical help to teens who want to experience true freedom in Christ.

Dear Reader:

We would appreciate hearing from you regarding this Harvest House nonfiction book. It will enable us to continue to give you the best in Christian publishing.

1. What most influenced you to purchase *The Seduction of Our Children*?
   - ❑ Author
   - ❑ Subject matter
   - ❑ Backcover copy
   - ❑ Recommendations
   - ❑ Cover/Title
   - ❑ _____

2. Where did you purchase this book?
   - ❑ Christian bookstore
   - ❑ General bookstore
   - ❑ Department store
   - ❑ Grocery store
   - ❑ Other

3. Your overall rating of this book:
   - ❑ Excellent ❑ Very good ❑ Good ❑ Fair ❑ Poor

4. How likely would you be to purchase other books by this author?
   - ❑ Very likely
   - ❑ Somewhat likely
   - ❑ Not very likely
   - ❑ Not at all

5. What types of books most interest you? (check all that apply)
   - ❑ Women's Books
   - ❑ Marriage Books
   - ❑ Current Issues
   - ❑ Christian Living
   - ❑ Bible Studies
   - ❑ Fiction
   - ❑ Biographies
   - ❑ Children's Books
   - ❑ Youth Books
   - ❑ Other _____

6. Please check the box next to your age group.
   - ❑ Under 18
   - ❑ 18-24
   - ❑ 25-34
   - ❑ 35-44
   - ❑ 45-54
   - ❑ 55 and over

Mail to: Editorial Director
Harvest House Publishers
1075 Arrowsmith
Eugene, OR 97402

Name _____

Address _____

City _____ State _____ Zip _____

**Thank you for helping us to help you
in future publications!**